BE A CHRISTIAN WARRIOR

You Are Chosen!

JOHN 15:19

PREPARE TO TRIUMPH IN A FALLEN WORLD

By Martin Mawyer

With Jerry Skirvin

PUBLISHED BY PRB PUBLISHING

BE A CHRISTIAN WARRIOR
(First in a Series)

YOU ARE CHOSEN!
PREPARE TO TRIUMPH IN A FALLEN WORLD

Published by PRB Publishing.

ISBN-13:
978-0-578-58044-9

Printed in the United States of America.

Cover Design:
Robert J. Kirchman

Editorial Consultant:
Alec Rooney

Interior Design & Layout:
Patti A. Pierucci

We, the authors, dedicate this book to
David William T. Carroll, whose friendship,
advice and support has both blessed and enriched
our lives for many wonderful decades.

TABLE OF CONTENTS

INTRODUCTION

I have chosen you out of the world, therefore the world hateth you.

(John 15:19)

With the very rare exception, it is exciting to be *chosen*. Being chosen gives us a sense of self-worth, acceptance, competence. On the other hand, being told to "get out," "scram" or that we are "not qualified" leaves us feeling rejected and inept. To be chosen means we have something to offer, something maybe not found in others, that we have the necessary skills to compete, and that our abilities can help achieve an important task.

Jesus said, "For many are called, but few are chosen." (Matt. 22:14)

Those words describe life, do they not? Throughout our lives we answer calls that often lead to rejection. Hundreds show up at Hollywood casting calls; only a few are selected. Dozens show up at sporting tryouts, where sometimes no one qualifies. Only two percent of job applicants who respond to an employment ad ever get an interview, much less the job. Of the 34,295 student applicants seeking admission to Harvard University in 2018, only 5.9 percent (2,023) were chosen. Such is life. It's a hard reality. Rejection happens more often than selection.

So why should we be surprised that Jesus said he has called many, but only a few are chosen?

In this earthly realm, it is sometimes difficult to maintain our excitement if we are *chosen*. But how exciting would it be if Christ—the King of Kings—chose us? After all, we did not petition Christ. Instead, Christ looked down upon the many whom were called and for some reason … He chose us!

"You did not choose me, I chose you," Christ says in John 15:16.

But … chosen for what? It most certainly isn't to warm a bench while others do all the work.

Employers do not choose job applicants to sit at their desks and twiddle their thumbs all day. Athletic teams do not choose players who have no ability or drive to compete. Universities do not choose applicants who have no intention of graduating.

The very nature of the word "chosen" implies that the chosen person has the responsibility to do something, to contribute.

Christ does not choose a person for the purpose of salvation, though it is a reward of being chosen. Christians are not chosen for the purpose of shaking sin out of their lives; sin could even destroy the reason for being chosen. Christians are not chosen for the purpose of loving one another, though without love we would never succeed in our chosen mission.

Often we make the mistake of thinking that we were chosen just so we could bear the fruits of the spirit—love, joy, peace, forbearance, kindness, goodness, faithfulness, gentleness and self-control. (Gal. 5:22)

We all need to cultivate these fruits for the task ahead, but they are not *why* we were chosen. A sandlot baseball team does not choose a player simply because he or she has the right equipment—bat, glove, cap, ball, uniform and cleats. That person is chosen because he is expected to *do* something with all that equipment while wearing that apparel.

Having the right equipment is great, but it is not an end unto itself. What is the point of all that equipment if you are not going to use it? That gear was given to us so we can serve the Kingdom of God—a kingdom that continually confronts violence, as will be explained later—and so that we can effectively be a light to the world and be the salt of the earth.

That is why we were chosen.

In a 2019 article in the *Christian Post*, Senior Pastor Robbie Gallaty of Long Hollow Baptist Church in Hendersonville, Tenn., says most churches are preaching only half the gospel. That is true.

Gallaty says churches "rarely think about the kingdom, much less speak about it."

The kingdom was the predominant topic that Jesus Christ spoke about, he writes.

"If the purpose of Christianity is just to enter heaven, Jesus wouldn't have left us on Earth after He saved us. We'd be raptured without a second to spare to enjoy eternity with Him. Surely the purpose of the kingdom of heaven is greater than just achieving eternal life," Gallaty writes. Those who want to explore this important message more deeply can find it in his book *Here And Now: Thriving in the Kingdom of Heaven Today*. (B&H, 2019).

Preaching about and defending the Kingdom of God, which incorporates being a light to the world and the salt of the earth, is not easy—especially in today's hostile climate toward Christians.

But despite the difficulties, that is the very purpose for which we have been chosen.

The enemies of God, those antichrists that have existed since the birth of our Savior, have also been chosen for a purpose: They want to destroy God's Kingdom. Opposing these evildoers and defending the Kingdom will a take a fully equipped soldier of Christ.

The purpose of this book is to equip you, as that soldier of Christ, for triumph in a world that is becoming increasingly hostile toward Christian believers.

We will explore testimonials, scripture, personal experience, examples and historical accounts to guide the reader through the often difficult and challenging work of defending God's Kingdom.

The format of this book follows that of other reputable guides: What is the problem? Who caused the problem? What is at stake? How should one respond? What are the risks? What is being defended? How does one prepare oneself? What is our objective? What equipment is needed? How do we engage?

This could be a journey like no other you have experienced.

While I am the primary author of this book, the manuscript would not have been possible without the help of co-author Jerry Skirvin, whose insight, direction, experience and guidance proved invaluable.

Just about anyone can put words on paper and claim to have written a book, just as a lyricist can write down words and claim to have written a song. But without the music, the beat, the tempo or the instruments, the work will be incomplete. For these reasons I am forever grateful and indebted to Jerry. His dedicated persistence and tireless efforts have provided the cadence, inspiration and tone that a subject of this magnitude and importance so desperately needs.

Jerry and I have been on the front lines in defending the truths, values, morals and eternal teachings of the Kingdom of God for more than 40 years apiece. Jerry has worked alongside some of the most influential figures in the pro-family, pro-life and pro-Bible movement, starting as an assistant to Dr. Jerry Falwell, who founded the Moral Majority in 1979. This was where I first met Jerry, after following Dr. Falwell's invitation to become editor of his *Moral Majority Report.*

Our careers took different paths during those four decades, with Jerry helping the causes of Col. Oliver North, the Rutherford Institute, Liberty Council and many other effective pro-family organizations and leaders. My path was slightly different; I founded the Christian Action Network in 1990, wanting to blaze my own trail as another separate and loud voice opposing and exposing evil.

> *"What I tell you in the darkness, speak in the light; and what you hear whispered in your ear, proclaim upon the housetops." (Matt. 10:27 NASB)*

Through those combined 80 years of experience, Jerry and I have fought many battles, learned many lessons and, at times, experienced the joy of successfully defending God's Kingdom as soldiers of Christ.

This book is a culmination of what we have learned about achieving triumph in a world hostile toward Christians. The reader, we believe, will be blessed to learn from our experiences, hardships and lessons. Most importantly, the reader will gain insight and understanding into the many scriptural principals needed to realize that success.

As a final note before you begin to equip yourself as a warrior of Christ, it should be mentioned that this book presents numerous examples of how Christianity is actively under attack in the United States. The status of some of these cases may have changed by the time you are reading these words, but the examples they provide are still useful and instructive. No doubt as one example fades into history, many more—possibly with more severe implications—will come to center stage. This should serve as a reminder that nothing really disappears from history, and that we need to heed philosopher George Santayana's famous warning: "Those who do not remember the past are condemned to repeat it."

You Are Chosen! is the first book in a series called *Be A Christian Warrior.* The next book in the series, God willing, will be titled *Salt and Light* and will focus on how Christians can reclaim the very first command God gave to man: To subdue and rule the earth. Though the next book will stand on its own, *You Are Chosen!* will lead the reader to an understanding as to why God gave us that task and what we must do to prepare for it, embrace it and fulfill it.

—*Martin Mawyer*

Unless otherwise noted, all scripture references are from the King James Bible.

CHAPTER ONE:

WE ARE
UNDER ATTACK

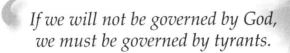

*If we will not be governed by God,
we must be governed by tyrants.*

It has been disputed whether William Penn, the noted English Quaker who founded the Province of Pennsylvania, ever actually wrote or spoke this famous phrase. It never appears in any of Penn's historical writings.

The quote also appears in different forms, though it is always basically the same idea: If men and women refuse to govern themselves with God as their guide, then they will be ruled by other men and women more powerful than themselves.

There are many common epigrams in our culture that are misquotes or mutations of the originals. Others have been simplified so modern society can digest them better.

For example, Paul Revere never yelled, "The British are coming!" He said something much more colloquial during his midnight ride to alert colonial militia of advancing British soldiers. "The regulars are coming out!" he called from his horse.

George Washington's "I cannot tell a lie?" Every adult knows he never confessed to chopping down a cherry tree. It's fiction. But it is also a venerable maxim that has served well over the years to teach children not to lie.

Or take the phrase, "Blood is thicker than water." The original version is: "The blood of the covenant is thicker than the water of the womb." Why not use five words instead of thirteen? Shorter seems better, catchier.

Ever heard the phrase, "Nice guys finish last"? The source of that famous quote is baseball legend and hall-of-famer Leo Durocher. The bombastic former Yankee manager was also known as "Leo the Lip,"

In 2017 this bench was removed from a park in Pennsylvania after a court ruled it was too religious.

and for good reason. In 1945 Baseball Commissioner Happy Chandler suspended him for an entire year over his on-field tantrums. The commissioner was fed up with Durocher's "accumulation of unpleasant incidents detrimental to baseball." Given his often sour disposition, it made sense that he would probably have said something like "Nice guys finish last," but he disputes ever having said it. "I never did say that you can't be a nice guy and win," Durocher once objected. "I said that if I was playing third base and my mother rounded third with the winning run, I'd trip her up." Poor mom.

Most of these supposedly historical quotes have one thing in common, one thing that makes them so celebrated (even if modified): They each contain an element of truth. Does it really matter if we shorten them and make them snappier?

Can you guess how this next quote was shortened?

"When bad men combine, the good must associate; else they will fall one by one, an unpitied sacrifice in contemptible struggle."

Huh?

This is a quote from Edmund Burke, the father of conservatism. Thankfully, it has been simplified to: "The only thing necessary for the triumph of evil is for good men to do nothing."'

That is not only easier to grasp, but also more powerful!

So William Penn probably never said, scribbled or mumbled the phrase, "If we will not be governed by God, we must be governed by tyrants." Yet it will eternally belong to him. President Ronald Reagan attributed the words to Penn in his well-known 1983 "Evil Empire" speech. If it's good enough for The Gipper, shouldn't it be good enough for history?

The quote was once emblazoned on a park bench in Oil City, Pa., but was deemed too religious by an atheist group and—in what might be considered an act of tyranny all its own—a court ruled in May 2017 that the bench be removed from public sight.

Ironically, the banishment of the bench actually helps prove the point of the quote. If God does not govern us, then tyrants—other people—will rule us.

Regardless of liberal attempts to stamp it out, Penn's proverb will continue to live on in history because it has a message rooted in truth. With each passing day in America, we are watching that truth become a nightmarish reality.

Again, it bears repeating: *If we will not be governed by God, we must be governed by tyrants.*

Anti-religious tyrants are hell-bent on destroying personal liberties, freedoms and God-given rights. They would prefer to be the ones who rule us.

Though they cloak themselves in tolerance, peace, equality and diversity, in reality they wear the "last days" chains of 2 Timothy 3:2-4:

> *"For men will be lovers of themselves, lovers of money, boasters, proud, blasphemers, disobedient to parents, unthankful, unholy, unloving, unforgiving, slanderers, without self-control, brutal, despisers of good, traitors, headstrong, haughty, lovers of pleasure rather than lovers of God, having a form of godliness but denying its power."*

Let's not forget to add verse seven as a link to their shackles of impertinence: "Always learning and never able to come to the knowledge of the truth.

The Antichrists are Already Here

Even though Timothy had an exhaustive laundry list of foul behavior that consumes the last days of man, there is one ugly trait he left out: Self-righteousness. The self-righteous believe they are far more intelligent, clever, educated and enlightened than old-fashioned Christians, whom they view as backward, dogmatic, low-bred and driven by a boorish, dictatorial God.

Evolutionary biologist Richard Dawkins personifies this contempt for Christianity, so much so that he could be its poster child. In his book *The God Delusion*, Dawkins sums up his view of the Christian God like this:

> *"The God of the Old Testament is arguably the most un-pleasant character in all fiction: jealous and proud of it; a petty, unjust, unforgiving control-freak; a vindictive, blood-thirsty ethnic cleanser; a misogynistic, homophobic, racist, infanticidal, genocidal, filicidal, pestilential, megalomania-cal, sadomasochistic, capriciously malevolent bully."*

One wonders what he has to say about Satan.

Dawkins and his ilk clearly think Christians are fools, to which the Apostle Paul has already provided a rebuttal:

> *"But God hath chosen the foolish things of the world to con-found the wise; and God hath chosen the weak things of the world to confound the things which are mighty." (1 Cor. 1:27)*

There is no single, authoritative definition of who constitutes the "last days" men. Some are atheists. Some are secularists, humanists and agnostics. They can fall into categories of liberals, leftists and pro-gressives. They can be self-described as feminists, reformists and ra-tionalists. Some have no category. They are just angry, heartless, misguided people who feel it is their mission to destroy the kingdom of God.

Certainly not everyone in these groupings is a "last days" man; some are just confused, caught up in a web of deception. They do, however, have one thing in common: They are self-righteous in think-ing they have knowledge of truth that is higher and better than the truth of God, whom they believe is either nonexistent, dead, irrelevant or can somehow be refashioned and reformed.

As such, they take the form of the Antichrist:

> *"Let no one deceive you by any means; for that Day will not come unless the falling away comes first, and the man of sin is revealed, the son of perdition, who opposes and exalts himself above all that is called God or that is worshiped, so that he sits as God in the temple of God, showing himself that he is God." (2 Thes. 2:3-4)*

In fact, they themselves *are* antichrists, and they have been hanging around for a very long time:

> *"Little children, it is the last hour; and as you have heard that the Antichrist is coming, **even now many antichrists have come**, by which we know that it is the last hour." (1 John 18, emphasis added)*

The definition of these antichrists is very clear and precise: "He is antichrist who denies the Father and the Son." (1 John 2:22)

Are you waiting for the Antichrist to come? Stop waiting. The Apostle John says they are already here:

> *"Every spirit that does not confess that Jesus Christ has come in the flesh is not of God. **And this is the spirit of the Antichrist,** which you have heard was coming, and is now **already in the world." (1 John 4:3, emphasis added)***

So these antichrists have existed from the time of Jesus to the present day. When you wake up tomorrow, they will still be here.

During the end times, these antichrists will find their future leaders, as revealed in Revelations, in the False Prophet, the Beast and the Dragon. They will rule with ferocious tyranny.

Society's Need for Religious Principle

Tyranny is to be expected when people concoct their own laws, morals, social norms and human rights. If people reject the authority of a higher, heavenly power, then they get to choose for themselves what is right or wrong. The boundaries of their behavior are shaped and limited only by their own selfish ambitions and desires.

Patrick Henry, one of America's most revered Founding Fathers, viewed the dissemination of Christianity as vital to the proper management of society. In his pamphlet *A Bill for Establishing a Provision for Teachers of the Christian Religion* (January 1784), he wrote: "The general diffusion of Christian knowledge hath a natural tendency to correct the morals of men, restrain their vices, and preserve the people of society."

Some years later, President George Washington would publicly agree, stating in his 1796 Farewell Address, " ... reason and experience both forbid us to expect that national morality can prevail in exclusion of religious principle. It is substantially true that virtue or morality is a necessary spring of popular government."

The lack of a supreme, uniform code of good and evil will naturally lead to chaos and anarchy. A million people will have a million different versions of acceptable manners, rights, morality, rules of conduct and human re-sponsibility. In fact, such craziness is al-ready on display throughout America.

During the 2017 presidential inauguration of Donald Trump, feminist groups swarmed Capitol Hill by the thousands wearing peculiar pink hats. The hats were intended to represent female genitalia, a visual symbol they hoped would shock onlookers into accepting their claim that women are being oppressed in America.

Madonna, musing about "blowing up the White House," during the 2017 presidential inauguration.

From a grand podium on that rainy day in D.C., over-the-hill pop singer Madonna stood tall as she addressed nearly 200,000 pink-hatted protesters. She called for a violent revolution against Donald Trump, even saying, "I have thought an awful lot about blowing up the White House." Just a few moments later, apparently forgetting that she had just called for a deadly bombing against the White House, she proclaimed, "We choose love. We choose love. We choose love."

Love ... and bombs? Bombs that destroy peace and property and tear people limb from limb? The combined statements were about as contradictory as her adopted name, for she certainly is no Madonna. She does wear the moniker "Material Girl" brilliantly, however.

In the end, the feminist gathering was no more than a parade of blind, furious people that the rain could not wash away or cleanse.

A few days later another liberal group (with their own peculiar idea of what is right and wrong) blasted the women's march for their audacity in claiming that a person has to have female genitalia to be a woman.

Speaking for the transgender community, Taylor Griggs called it an "oppressive message" to say that "having a vagina is essential for womanhood." Sex organs and female chromosomes do not make a woman, went the argument; gender is determined by a person's conscious preference.

According to the nonprofit Human Rights Campaign, gender is "One's innermost concept of self as male, female, a blend of both or neither." So a person can be female, male, both or neither depending on their murky "innermost concept."

The venerable Princeton University has embraced this nonsense, now allowing students to select from six different gender identities: Cisgender, Genderqueer, Gender non-conforming, Transgender, Man, Woman and Other.

If that is not ridiculous enough, Facebook once had 71 gender options for people to choose from when setting up a profile page. For the sake of space and mercy toward the reader, those options will not be listed here.

So the "last days" man is not only willing to throw God out the window when determining standards of conduct, social norms, ethics, morality or even gender, he is equally willing to toss out scientific and secular standards like biology, genetics, history and, most alarmingly, common sense.

The Bible couldn't be any clearer on this issue; witness what Jesus told the Pharisees:

> *"And he answered and said unto them, Have ye not read,*
> *that he which made them at the beginning made them male*
> *and female." (Matt. 19:4)*

So on the one hand, feminists believe they are being oppressed for having female anatomy. On the other hand, transsexuals believe it is oppressive to say that a girl has to have female anatomy to be a woman. This is nonsense and tortured logic. One nearly has to deform one's brain just to make any sense of it.

No wonder these people can't see God. They can't see the physical difference between a male and a female!

If people are left to their own imaginations in deciding right and wrong, societal "truth" will be determined by whoever can shout the loudest and whoever has the power to silence the "truth" of someone else. When debate is not enough to decide arguments, when the "meeting of the minds" is impossible, when calm persuasion comes up empty, when gentle coercion becomes fruitless, tyranny crouches in the background like a jaguar patiently stalking its prey. Right now that predator has its gaze fixed on God's people.

The 'Last Days' in America

We see this happening across America as the "last days" man attempts to eradicate, reshape, deny and disgrace American traditions, history, culture and religion — all because these virtues interfere with the elevation and promotion of their new alt-truths.

Evidence of this can be found almost nightly on the news. U.S. flags have been forcibly removed from properties of homeowners. Religious symbols have been yanked from public view. Historical monuments have been uprooted and placed in storage lockers. All under a new set of "fairer" rules that are being relentlessly forced upon us.

Conservatives have had their speaking events canceled, their broadcasting careers ruined and their television shows canceled because they have expressed negative opinions on homosexual marriage or Islam. Liberals have burned conservative books, removed historical texts from school libraries and denied conservative clubs the right to organize on college campuses, calling them racist, oppressively religious or hateful. Brand names have been pulled from sports teams with "offensive" mascots; public schools, government buildings and products have been renamed because someone finds their namesakes' history or political orientation offensive.

Most of these silencing and censoring efforts have been accomplished through public shaming or through organized protests or lawsuits, with ample help from an ever-complicit news media.

When peaceful means fail, or when the anarchists are not patient enough to wade through traditional outlets for outrage, they use violence or the threat of violence to try and suppress truths they don't want others to hear.

This is what happened in February 2017 when protesters gathered at the University of California

Conservative commentator Milo Yiannopoulos.

at Berkeley ahead of a speech by conservative commentator Milo Yiannopoulos. The violence (which included the flinging of rocks, fireworks and Molotov cocktails) resulted in more than $100,000 worth of property damage to the university.

The use of actual violence makes even the *threat* of violence into a more effective tool for the "last days" man to suppress conservative truths. At the same university, conservative writer and commentator Ann Coulter's appearance was canceled less than two months later when protesters announced they would renew violence if she were allowed to speak. No rocks or Molotov cocktails were even required by that point.

When something as basic, time-honored and cemented in American history as a person's free-speech rights are routinely revoked by a mob, then this is tyranny.

Just What is Tyranny?

There is no universal definition of a tyrant or tyranny. They can range from a military dictatorship to a single, absolute ruler. Tyranny can even spring from democracy, which President John Adams called the "tyranny of the majority." (That's like the famous case of two foxes and a chicken voting on what's for dinner.)

Alexander Hamilton, a Founding Father of the United States, was equally if not more condemnatory of the "tyranny of the majority." In a speech urging the ratification of the U.S. Constitution, Hamilton said a pure democracy might seem to be a perfect government. But a pure democracy has in the end, he warned, always led to tyranny.

"A pure democracy, if it were practicable," said Hamilton, "would be the most perfect government. Experience has proved that no position is *more false* than this ... Their very character was tyranny." (June 21, 1788, emphasis added)

Of all the various political forces that could prop up tyranny in the United States, the tyranny of the majority should concern us the most.

It was this concern that prompted the framers of the U.S. Constitution to create the Bill of Rights. Supposedly, even a majority of people would not have the power or means to infringe on certain inalienable rights—free speech being one of the most basic and fundamental and therefore needing to be enshrined in the First Amendment.

But the "last days" man—those little antichrists—want *their* truths to rule America and not those Biblical truths that have guided American law, social norms, traditions and morality for more than two centuries.

To successfully impose these imaginary, man-made truths on others, the "last days" man must practice tyranny. He must deconstruct certain sections of the Bill of Rights, with the right to bear arms, free speech and religious freedom topping the list since they are all natural obstacles to the "last days" man. If these sections can be obliterated, or at least watered down, then the tyranny of the majority can rule unchallenged.

CHAPTER TWO:

HOW IS THE ATTACK UNFOLDING?

In righteousness you will be established: Tyranny will be far from you; you will have nothing to fear. Terror will be far removed; it will not come near you.

(Isa. 54:14 NIV)

Tyranny comes in three stages, stages which can overlap as the oppression progresses.

The First Stage of Tyranny

The first stage of tyranny, as we discussed in Chapter One, is to silence opposing views or truths.

Typical tools include enforcing political correctness; targeting groups, corporations and people for retribution; and shaming opponents as "hatemongers," "-phobes," "racists," "fascists" and yes, even as a "basket of deplorables."

Shaming is an effective tool for silencing opposing opinions. It seeks to make people into social pariahs and causes them to be ostracized in public, on the job and even at home. No human likes being rejected, shunned or dismissed. Who wants to stand at the water cooler alone, or watch friends back away or roll their eyes, or be the subject of disapproving whispers among co-workers? The whole point of shaming is to isolate a person and make an embarrassment of his opinions, beliefs and actions.

Though shaming tactics are mostly directed at individuals, they can be used against bigger targets as well. Television stations, news and entertainment operations, publishers, educational institutions and social media platforms have all been shamed for giving conservatives a voice.

Big and small businesses, colleges and universities, sports franchises, clubs, organizations and even families have been targeted for retribution if they are found to be connected or identified in any way with a conservative position.

Corporations have been attacked simply for placing product advertisements on conservative talk show programs. Hotels have been threatened for hosting conservative events and speakers. Family members have been pilloried because of political views held by spouses, siblings or parents.

America witnessed examples of such assaults against family members shortly after President Trump was inaugurated.

Saturday Night Live tastelessly claimed that Trump's school-age son, Barron, could become America's "first homeschool shooter." Rosie O'Donnell suggested that Barron was autistic. The *Daily Mail* newspaper claimed Melania Trump was a prostitute. The *Daily Show* even pushed the idea that President Trump wants to have sex with his own daughter, Ivanka. (Liberals also called for a boycott of Ivanka-line products.) And let's not forget the aging Madonna's spoken desire to blow up the White House (and presumably anyone unlucky enough to be inside) because it gives President Trump a platform to promote his version of truth.

Shutting Us Up, Shutting Us Down

Shaming tactics have been used to get conservatives fired from their jobs and to deny them the right even to have jobs in certain professions, especially if those professions interact with the public. Courts have been used to suppress conservative truths if someone influential deems those truths exclusionary or "judgmental." Even law enforcement has been used to gag and shame conservative opinions.

In 2010 I was in New York City showing the Christian Action Network's documentary film about 9/11 family members and their opposition to a mosque slated for construction at the site of the destroyed World Trade Center. We showed our film outdoors on a big, inflatable screen in the night air of Washington Square Park in Lower Manhattan. About halfway through the public showing I found myself surrounded by several police officers. They seemed just as nonplussed as

I was for having been called to the scene.

They asked to see my event permit, which I showed them. Finding nothing wrong with the permit, they approached a crowd of New York University students who were shouting, "Hate speech! Hate speech!"

"Who called the police?" one officer yelled above the angry crowd. A couple of young male students came forward and indicated they had.

"What's the problem?" another officer asked.

"They're committing hate speech," one of the students answered.

The officers pulled the two men aside and calmly told them that speech is not crime.

"But they're saying hateful things about Muslims," one of the students persisted.

Of course, we weren't. Our film consisted of nothing but interviews of 9/11 family members whose loved ones had been murdered by Muslim terrorists who attacked New York City in September of 2001. The families were understandably outraged that a mosque was being planned for the very site where their loved ones had been brutally and publicly slain … in the name of Islam. To hand such a site even partially over to the worship of Allah was to these people an incredibly painful insult.

"I don't know what's in this film and I don't care," one officer explained. "They have a permit and there's no such thing as a 'hate speech' crime. We can't and we won't stop them from showing their film. They have a permit."

We finished our screening, but not without several angry protesters shouting in our faces until the event was over. It was an absolutely perfect example of a tyrannical mob trying to twist the law to silence free speech.

Antifa: The Left Gets Nasty

Tyrannical mobs are unfortunately now becoming institutionalized in America, with two violent, far-left groups gaining national prominence: Antifa and By Any Means Necessary. Often these two groups show up at the same event and coordinate their violent behavior.

Antifa, rioting at UC Berkeley in 2017.

Antifa (for "anti-fascist") finds its roots in Europe, going back to the early 20th century when it was formed to oppose fascist regimes. Over the decades its importance declined with the fading of fascism on the Continent. Rather than fade away into obscurity, however, it proceeded to redefine fascism as any truth, leader, political group or movement that goes against its rigid political leanings, which are to the left of far-left.

Do you oppose homosexuality? Then you're a *homophobe*. Do you oppose radical Islam? Then you are a *Nazi*. Do you own a Confederate flag? Then you are a *racist*. Do you support capitalism or question labor unions? Then you are a *fascist*. Do you think America is exceptional? Then you are a *white nationalist*.

They often sport banners at their demonstrations that read: "The Only Good Fascist is a Dead One." Sure enough, this vitriolic name-calling and provocation indicates Antifa's willingness to commit real, physical violence against its opponents.

Antifa was behind the violent, destructive attacks at UC Berkeley in 2017, where conservative commentator Milo Yiannopoulos had been scheduled to speak, as described in Chapter One.

They were in Hamburg, Germany in July of the same year, protesting the G-20 Summit, an important gathering of world leaders. Supposedly angry over capitalism and environmental issues, Antifa and their fellow conspirators set cars on fire, looted stores, threw petrol bombs, terrorized residents and injured more than 200 police officers.

They were in Washington, D.C. during the inauguration of President Trump, dressed in black. They broke windows, set a limousine on fire and made a failed attempt to set off foul-smelling butyric acid bombs in the ventilation system of the National Press Club, which was hosting a Trump celebration.

They also appeared in Philadelphia, Pa., where they not only attacked demonstrators protesting radical Islam but made attacks on police, including stabbing a horse. At a Portland, Ore. demonstration, police seized clubs, canisters of mace, knives, hammers, batons and even brass knuckles from Antifa members.

The group consists mostly of college students and teenagers whose stated goal is to "smash fascism in all its forms."

Echoes from the Bible

There is nothing new about Antifa's strategy of smearing opponents with false accusations and derogatory words, and then using those allegations to justify violence.

This is, in fact, exactly what happened to Jesus Christ. The Sanhedrin brought perjurers against Christ to justify handing Him over to Pontius Pilate. Pilate was not fooled. He knew the real reason was envy. He even asked the angry mob, "What evil has He done?" Of course it was too late. The horde had pushed into an emotional frenzy, whipped up by the chief priests. More falsehoods were thrown out, like the claim that Jesus forbade paying taxes to Caesar and that He claimed to be a king. Pilate, unmoved and dismissive of the charges, actually defended Jesus. "I find no fault in this Man," he said. They shouted back, "Let Him be crucified." An indignant Pilate at first refused to listen, and then washed his hands of the matter: "You take Him and crucify Him, for I find no fault in Him."

Then Jesus' accusers used what liberals are so fond of using today: circular reasoning or begging the question: "If you let this Man go, you are not Caesar's friend. Whoever makes himself a king speaks against Caesar" (John 19:12). Looking over the crowd, Pilate saw a riot taking shape.

The process was complete. Pilate ordered Christ crucified.

We have seen Antifa's strategy before. It's as old as the trial and death of Christ: Make false accusations. Whip up the crowd. Reach unfounded conclusions based on false assertions. Start riots and violence.

The left also loves to use guilt by association to demonize its opponents. An illustration of this (among many others that could be recounted here) is when Democratic Congresswoman Kathleen Rice outrageously claimed in August 2017 that NRA members "are quickly becoming domestic security threats."

Why? Because the NRA supports gun ownership of course, and guns are used to commit crimes and hurt people. It does not matter to Rice that guns are an individual's ultimate defense against abusive, oppressive government (probably at the center of her real problem with them). Guns can be used to do bad things, her argument goes, so the NRA consists of bad people, period.

She had no foundation for her accusation, and offered no examples of NRA members becoming security threats. She couldn't cite a single statement where the NRA made such a threat. Yet she put the falsehood out there, not only to help set the stage for abolishing gun rights, but to justify committing acts violence against NRA members, merely by virtue of their association with firearms.

The Second Stage of Tyranny

The second stage of tyranny, following efforts to silence opposing voices through shaming, intimidation and violence, is to actually criminalize speech that supports opposing opinions. This process is also well under way in America.

For more than two decades, pro-life protesters have been arrested outside abortion clinics for claiming that life begins at conception.

Street preachers have been arrested for openly sharing their faith, as in the case of Todd Leibovitz in San Antonio, Texas, who spent a night in jail for sharing passages from the Bible on a public sidewalk.

In Battle Creek, Mich., three students were arrested for handing out copies of the U.S. Constitution on college property.

At a Los Angeles VA facility, a 74-year-old U.S. Army veteran was arrested for posting two American flags on a fence.

Campus police at the University of Texas issued a citation against an outdoor preacher for speaking against homosexual sex. In fact the preacher was not even on campus property while making the speech; he was across the street. That did not matter. His voice carried far enough onto university grounds for students to hear and that was enough to get him a citation. He was told that it was illegal to offend university students.

It's like a new twist on the old adage, "If you can't do the time, don't do the crime." The University of Texas might also tell you: "If you can't pay the fine, don't speak your mind."

Mind the Snowflakes

This notion has spread like wildfire among young people across American college and university campuses—the belief that *it is criminal to offend someone else.* This should give us pause. Many of these students are likely the future leaders and lawmakers of America.

Many college students are now living in a culture built on emotional weakness. For this reason, among others, they have been labeled as "snowflakes," convinced of their own inherent beautiful specialness and ready to melt at the slightest offense. The policies of some universities have done nothing to dispel this notion and in fact they encourage it.

The student handbook at the University of Arizona tells students to scream "ouch" if they are offended. The University of Florida, during the celebration of Halloween, has an emergency hotline for students to call if they are forced to look upon a costume they find offensive. At the University of Mississippi, the annual "A Grand ole Christmas" tree-lighting ceremony was thought to be bruising some feelings because it "connoted too much Christianity on campus." It was changed to "Hotty Toddy Holiday."

These incidents are just a few examples among many, and illustrate how laws, ordinances and policies are being changed and used to shut down opposing views, especially those that are Biblically founded.

And while many of these types of cases are based on local or state law, there's a growing push for federal laws that would criminalize "offending" speech, an effort that is gaining traction.

One absurd case took place in Bernards Township, N.J., during a public hearing on the construction of a community mosque. A federal judge in August, 2017, ordered that residents were not allowed to discuss the topics of "Islam" or "Muslims" during the debate.

"No commentary regarding Islam or Muslims will be permitted," the court ruled.

Prior restraint? Chilling effect? Free speech violation? The judge threw all of the legal protections afforded ordinary citizens to freely engage in public discourse right out the window.

Already the federal government can arrest people for *Civil Rights Intimidation.* It is clever way of skirting the First Amendment's protection of free speech by making it a crime to say something that might "intimidate" another person. We are not talking about someone issuing a physical threat and wanting to do bodily harm (which *is* against the law and not protected speech). Rather *Civil Rights Intimidation* is speech that makes a person feel insecure, insulted or uncomfortable. It can be any speech or action that another considers a display of harassment or intolerance.

In short, it can be *anything you say.*

Obama Administration to the Rescue

In 2016, President Barack Obama established a special civil rights unit to ferret out such speech that others might consider "harassment." Headquartered in Boston, top prosecutors from eleven states are now on the prowl for offensive speech or activity. (The force so far remains in place under the Trump administration.)

Upon establishing the unit, then-U.S. Attorney General Loretta Lynch said, "There is no place for intolerance in our country." It was a broad, sweeping statement that gives federal authorities vast, undefined and capricious power to single out anyone thought to be intolerant, and to behave very intolerantly toward them.

To say "there is no place for intolerance in our country" is an absurd statement on its face. There is lots of room in America for intolerance. Do we tolerate rapists? Pedophiles? Swindlers? Sex traffickers? Even vandals, litterers or people who park illegally or scream obscenities in public places? Of course not.

What Attorney Lynch was really saying is there is "no place for intolerance in our country" of the new alt-truths of the radical left: homosexuality, global warming, abortion, gender neutrality, Islam, multiculturalism and environmentalism, to name a few. You are simply not allowed to disagree with those things, because the left says so.

The guiding language of the *Civil Rights Intimidation* unit says, "The unit will focus on enforcing those laws that prohibit discrimination and **harassment** on the basis of race, national origin, gender, religion ... " (Emphasis added. U.S. Attorney Carmen Ortiz, February 21, 2016, *The Daily Free Press*)

When the language says "those laws," it is referring to the Civil Rights Act of 1964, which specifically prohibits "discrimination" against certain classes of people. The problem is, the Civil Rights Act of 1964 does not include the word "harassment," which has been added to the language of the civil rights unit. The Obama Administration simply inserted that vague word, so open to interpretation, hoping no one would notice.

So rather than just enforcing laws that prohibit *discrimination*, the feds can now go after people who commit *harassment*. This means America now has a dedicated law enforcement agency on the hunt for anyone who may personally, verbally aggravate someone else or a class of people. This is much more sweeping than clamping down on discriminatory acts that deny segments of society jobs, public access, opportunities or benefits. This is an effort to criminalize *hurting someone's feelings*, to put words into the same category as actual weapons.

Turning Opinions into Crimes

This sneaky, troublesome use of the word "harassment" is an example of how the liberal left will expand, distort, misdirect, twist and abuse statutes to give themselves the additional weapons they need to silence opposing opinions.

Though there are many reasons to object to making it a crime to insult someone else, the dangers of the *Civil Rights Intimidation* unit go much deeper than what is immediately obvious.

The insult needs only to be subjective, not actual. In other words, if you proclaim a general opinion that makes someone feel uncomfortable or unsafe, then that is harassment and an act of intolerance—and criminal. For instance, saying publicly that Islam is an evil religion is not directed against anyone in particular. But if a Muslim hears the statement, he or she could claim to have felt harassed … and to have been subjected to intolerance.

A perfect example of this occurred in Pocatello, Idaho, in April of 2016. The case involved an unknown person placing dozens of DVDs on car windows at Idaho State University. The DVDs contained material that took a critical look at radical Islam. After university officials watched the content they determined it was offensive to Muslim students. They declared that distributing the DVDs was a civil rights violation even though they could cite nothing in the DVD that was untrue. The federal government was called in, and promptly set about wasting taxpayer money and resources to hunt down the lawless pamphleteer.

Then-U.S. Attorney Wendy Olson, who spearheaded the operation, arrived at the university with grim determination. Within days she had held a press conference and made the spectacular announcement that distributing the DVDs was a violation of the U.S. Constitution.

"Incidents of discrimination, **harassment** and violence directed against an entire community because of how they pray or where they pray or what their beliefs are, are at odds with our **Constitution** and our values," Olson said (emphasis added).

Out of the gate, Ms. Olson was being deceptive and dishonest with the public and the media. The DVD made no statement on how Muslims pray or where they pray. Neither did it advocate discrimination or violence against Muslims. She invented this hoping her colorful rhetoric (and sandwiching the word *harassment* between the words *discrimination* and *violence*) would somehow bolster her opinion that a crime had been committed with the anonymous placement of disposable plastic disks on windshields.

The stage is set. A person's speech does not have to be directed at any particular individual to be considered criminal harassment. It does not even have to contain an insult. It can simply be a series of factual news clippings, as was the case of this DVD at Idaho State University. If a person's speech raises unflattering questions, or dares to portray a segment of society in an unfavorable light, then it has crossed the line into criminal harassment.

It is easy to see the domino effect at work in this case: Education becomes criticism; criticism becomes harassment; harassment becomes criminal and crimes can bring punishment, such as jail. (As a side note, at the time of this writing, the Idaho DVD pamphleteer has not been found or identified.)

The Third Stage of Tyranny

Following the first stage of tyranny, silencing opposing voices, and the second stage, criminalizing opposing views, the next stage is to compel people to actively and personally support, implement and participate in the tyrants' newly minted "truths."

Government agencies, for instance, have attempted to force a bakery in Oregon to make a cake for a gay couple's wedding; a photography studio in New Mexico to provide photography services for a gay wedding; a wedding venue in New York to perform a homosexual marriage; a county clerk in Kentucky to issue a gay marriage license.

In each case individuals refused to provide services due to their Christian beliefs, and the result was fines, jail and/or re-education in sensitivity training classes.

It is rare in the United States that people are compelled to engage in behavior that violates their religious faith. Sure, history is replete with examples of people in other countries

Jack Phillips, a Colorado baker, was sued when he refused to bake a cake for a gay couple.

who have not been allowed to practice their faith or have been forced to do something in violation of their religious conscience, and those people are more often than not living under some form of outright tyranny.

Yet we are seeing this type of tyranny becoming a reality here in America, probably the last place on earth, the last form of government and the last type of people you would ever expect it to be coming from.

People living under tyranny can be forced to do many horrible and unimaginable things. We do not even have to examine modern-day history to find examples of this. We only need to look at the Bible and read the story of the Israelites when they were living in bondage under the tyranny of Egypt.

> *"Then the king of Egypt spoke to the Hebrew midwives, one of whom was named Shiphrah and the other was named Puah; and he said, 'When you are helping the Hebrew women to give birth and see them upon the birthstool, if it is a son, then you shall put him to death; but if it is a daughter, then she shall live.' " (Exodus 1:15-16 NASB)*

This Egyptian tyrant forced Hebrew midwives to become baby killers, because it served the purpose of the country.

The framers of our Constitution knew the dangers of tyranny, which is why they included the Bill of Rights. Fortunately the Bill of Rights includes the Second Amendment, which allows citizens to bear arms to defend themselves *against* government tyranny.

One Nation—and Government—Under God

There are significant societal advantages to having people believe in God-given biblical truths. Most importantly, everyone is looking at the same guidebook for right, wrong, justice, behavior, mercy and respect, to name a few shared virtues. These people are also aware that whatever they do is seen by and eventually answerable before God. This fosters self-regulated behavior.

> *" 'Can a man hide himself in hiding places so I do not see him?' declares the LORD. 'Do I not fill the heavens and the earth?'   declares the LORD." (Jeremiah 23:24 NASB)*

Not only does God hold the populace accountable; in a Godly society the government itself must stand before the same seat of judgment. An omnipotent God sets guidelines for the behavior of those who believe in Him, and this includes a nation's leaders. God never sleeps, so the people and their elected government know their actions are ultimately accountable before Him. Not only should people be held accountable to God, but the people should hold Government accountable to God.

Toss God aside and trash His universal and eternal truths, and everyone can decide to do what's right in his own eyes, as the Israelites did during the time of Judges:

"In those days there was no king in Israel; everyone did what was right in his own eyes." (Judges 21:25)

Without the fear of God, without universal truths, citizens and rulers alike will sink into their own preferences of right and wrong and behave and enact laws based solely on personal whim, gain and expediency. Such a society will eventually be sucked into a whirlpool of chaos and anarchy.

The result will be laws that are disagreeable not only to Christians but to non-Christians as well. In such a society, many will attempt to ignore, skirt or flout these contrived laws. The thirteen raucous years of the Prohibition era should serve as a satisfactory example of this inevitability. In trying to stamp out liquor, the country created bootleggers, gangsters, organized crime syndicates, dangerous speakeasies, poisonous alcohol and, probably most significantly, criminals out of ordinary citizens.

How often has it been said, "It's only a crime if I get caught"?

The thinking is, if God is not watching and the state is not watching, then who is there to catch or stop me from committing a crime? It is a good point (if it were ever true that God's not watching). Governments are never large enough to monitor every citizen continuously — at least not yet. If God is declared dead or viewed as nonexistent, then a nation's only hope of controlling an unruly population is fear, brute force and punishment. Of course secular governments do not start out brutal, because they initially govern under the myth that people are basically good and law abiding. The unruly few, they think, can be managed and the criminal can be prosecuted and incarcerated — and served up as a warning to others who may want to disobey.

Eventually they learn the truth, as God so clearly spelled out:

"And God saw that the wickedness of man was great in the earth, and that every imagination of the thoughts of his heart was only evil continually." (Gen. 6:5)

Jesus was more specific about the nature of man:

"For from within, out of the heart of men, proceed evil thoughts, adulteries, fornications, murders, thefts, covetousness, wickedness, deceit, lasciviousness, an evil eye, blasphemy, pride, foolishness: All these evil things come from within, and defile the man." (Mark 7:21-23 NASB)

If man's inclination is toward evil—continuous evil—then how can governments expect man to self-regulate his behavior without submission to God? They cannot. The eventual solution becomes harsh punishment, restrictions and surveillance. Enter tyranny.

The threat of tyranny should not be worrisome just to the godly, but to all those who act contrary to the whimsical, impulsive and flavor-of-the-month laws of a secular society.

Arbitrary and Capricious Laws

Here are a few examples of insane legal incidents that can affect Christian and non-Christian alike:

Armed agents of the Environmental Protection Agency (EPA) were dispatched to the home of Ashville, N.C., resident Larry Keller, simply over an email he sent to the regional administrator. In his 2012 message, he asked why the agency was trying to "crucify" executives of big oil and gas companies. The EPA did not like his use of the word "crucify," claiming it was threatening to their agents. Clearly this was not the case; Keller was simply repeating the very words used by EPA regional administrator Al Armendariz, who said in a YouTube clip that his enforcement philosophy was to "crucify" officials from big oil and gas companies. Dismissive of these openly available facts, the EPA confronted Keller with gun-toting agents. In reality, EPA officials were not in fear of their lives. They simply did not like being criticized. So they did what tyrants do best—they sent out armed agents to intimidate and silence the critic.

Few know that the EPA has more than 200 gun-carrying agents

equipped with body armor, camouflage equipment, unmanned aircraft, assault ships, radar and other military-style weaponry. One would think the EPA must be in a constant state of war. Of course they are not. These military-style resources just come in very handy when political enemies need to be silenced or intimidated.

America is witnessing huge growth in gun-toting federal agencies such as (believe it or not) the Department of Education, Social Security Administration and the Small Business Association. Even the National Institute of Standards and Technology (a federal agency that promotes innovation) has armed agents. In all, there are sixty-seven nonmilitary federal agencies that buy guns, ammunition and military-style equipment.

Interestingly, these armed federal agencies actually have very little use for weapons and body armor. This is why in fiscal years 2006-2014, these agencies spent $42 million allotted for guns and ammunition to instead purchase ping-pong balls, gym equipment, bread, copiers, cotton balls and cable television.

Nonetheless, the more sinister aspect remains. Agencies with armed agents sitting on their bottoms and twiddling their thumbs all day will eventually be put to work doing something—like perhaps intimidating the general populace, as happened to Larry Keller.

In one crazy case in Pinellas County, Fla., an environmental specialist showed up at the home of Scotty Jordan because smoke from his outdoor barbecue was wafting into his neighbor's yard. The environmental agent told Jordan that it was against the law for barbecue odor to leave his property.

"You're allowed to have it smell on your property, so that doesn't count," Agent Joe Graham told him. "But when I'm on the street, that's when it counts."

While standing on the street, Graham warned the homeowner, "I can smell it again right now." (The horror!) Graham issued Jordan a stern warning and nonsensically told him to confine his smoke to his own property in the future. Naturally the incident caused a national stink—a stink much fouler than the odor of Jordan's barbeque smoke.

In another example of tyrannical official overreach, two young sisters, aged seven and eight, had police show up at their home in Over-

Police in Overton, Texas, were called out to stop these sisters from from selling lemonade at their "illegal" lemonade stand.

ton, Texas, because they were operating an "illegal" lemonade stand. The apparent criminal enterprise began when the young girls decided to raise money to buy their dad a Father's Day present.

There are many more examples of heavy-handed, bureaucratic, monstrous laws and acts that have been used to compel people to either obey overzealous and liberal-activist inspired laws or to stop them from doing things that, in reality, no one should give a "Hotty Toddy" about.

Other examples (difficult to believe but real nonetheless) abound:

It is a crime in New York for people to take selfies with a lion, tiger or other big cat in the background. In Utah, it is a crime to collect rainwater on your own property. In Hilton Head Island, S.C., it is illegal to leave trash in your car.

The honor of topping the list of insane laws goes directly to the state of Georgia. It is illegal in that state to eat fried chicken with anything but your fingers. In 2009 Ginny Dietrick was celebrating her 91st birthday from out-of-state when she was arrested at the Longstreet Café in Gainesville for using a fork to eat her chicken. None other than the police chief himself, Frank Hopper, arrested her. The arrest was a prank and Dietrick was set free, but kudos to Sheriff Hopper for going to great lengths to demonstrate how stupid and ridiculous man's laws can become.

To think that our Declaration of Independence called England's King George III a "tyrant" who is "unfit to be the ruler of a free people." The American Revolution of 1776 happened over smaller acts of tyranny than what we are witnessing today in the United States.

Whether William Penn actually uttered his famous quote or not, the words are true:

"If we will not be governed by God, we must be governed by tyrants."

The Bible would never produce laws that would restrict citizens over innocuous emails, drifting barbecue smoke, unlicensed lemonade stands, photos with lions, having trash in one's car or collecting rainwater. (Not to mention displaying the American flag, speaking out against homosexuality or handing out the U.S. Constitution)

French philosopher Voltaire was no Christian. He was a deist, meaning his belief rested in a non-intervening God. Regardless of his religious views, he had a wisdom about tyranny that deserves our attention.

"If you want to know who controls you, look at who you are not allowed to criticize."

"It is dangerous to be right when the government is wrong."

"Those who can make you believe absurdities can make you commit atrocities."

And finally:

"So long as the people do not care to exercise their freedom, those who wish to tyrannize will do so."

Christ set us free. It is our inalienable right to be free in America, according to our Declaration of Independence. And as Christian warriors, it is our duty to maintain and defend those freedoms.

CHAPTER THREE:

HOW SHOULD THE ATTACK BE MET?

Peace on earth and good will toward men!
(Popular Christmas greeting)

Anyone growing up at a time when Christmas slogans graced city streets, store windows, parades and even schools will remember this famous quote attributed to the heralding angels at the time of Jesus' birth.

The quote was popular in hymns, storybooks and television shows. It could be found on Christmas cards, home decorations and bulbs dangling from evergreen trees. Back in the day when America actually celebrated religious words during Christmas, these cheering words could be seen and heard everywhere.

One can understand their popularity. Jesus Christ, a Savior to the world, was born and He was bringing with Him peace on earth and good will toward men. What could be more joyous, applauded or needed? The words are inspirational, calming, full of hope. They find their origin in the King James Version of the Bible:

> *"Glory to God in the highest, and on earth peace, good will toward men." (Luke 2:14)*

The problem is, much like the quote attributed to William Penn, the heralding angels never said it. The King James Version of this scripture is wrong. Jesus Christ did not come to bring peace on earth to *all* men. To argue that it is a correct interpretation puts it at odds with Matt. 10:34:

> *"Think not that I came to send peace on the earth: I came not to send peace, but a sword."*

So which is it? Is the traditional KJV rendering correct, that the angels declared the mission of Jesus was to bring "peace, good will toward men"? Or is Jesus deadly serious that his mission was *not* to "send peace, but a sword"? Either Jesus got it wrong or the angels got it wrong or the King James translators got it wrong.

We know the answer to this.

An Important Distinction

The King James Version of Luke 2:14 stands out as an oddity when compared to other Bible translations of the same verse. Most others say Jesus came to bring peace on earth and good will toward *men whom God favors or with whom He is well pleased.*

Typical of these translations is the New American Standard Bible (NASB), which says:

> *"Glory to God in the highest, And on earth peace among men **with whom He is pleased.**" (emphasis added)*

The variation in phraseology may appear to be insignificant at first glance, but upon closer examination there is a stark difference. The peace of which the angels spoke was peace between God and men *with whom He is pleased.* Where once we were enemies of God (Rom. 5:10), we are now at peace with Him through the saving grace of Jesus Christ. There is no peace between God, Jesus, and the Holy Spirit … and the unsaved.

The angels were not speaking about some utopian, ideal peace among *all* men on earth. If they were, then why would Jesus have warned that the earth would suffer through wars and rumors of wars? If Jesus came to bring peace to earth, then there would be no wars. Instead, Jesus said:

> *"You will be hearing of wars and rumors of wars. See that you are not frightened, for those things must take place, but that is not yet the end." (Matt. 24:6 NASB)*

Even a casual observer of world history knows that peace has never been the universal state of the Earth at any time.

So either Christ failed miserably in bringing peace or the KJV translators failed miserably in interpreting the scripture. The latter is the obvious correct answer. Not only did Christ *not* come to bring peace; He actually came to bring a sword.

This has been a challenging and tortured passage for Bible scholars and commentators. We associate Christ with love, mercy, forgiveness, acceptance and gentleness. While He certainly embodies all of these qualities, Christ is also adamant that He "came not to send peace, but a sword."

This is difficult for many churches and parishioners who preach and believe Jesus is nothing but a bundle of hugs and kisses and smiles whose only weapon is love. Jesus never said, "Love conquers all." That ubiquitous and clever coinage goes to the ancient Roman poet Virgil, who was a pagan. Such a concept and projection of Christ—as some sort of meek, docile pacifist who treats His enemies with open arms and warm embraces—is not only wrong but also scripturally unfounded.

Servants Who Perform vs. Those Who Do Not

Jesus was unmistakably talking about Himself as the executioner in the *Parable of the Minas*. (Luke 19:11-27) As a quick scripture reminder, Jesus tells the story of a nobleman who went into a far country to receive a kingdom and return. Clearly this is a parable of Christ receiving His heavenly kingdom and returning to earth.

As the nobleman was leaving, he asked ten of his servants to take a mina (a unit of currency) each to do business while he was gone. Nearly all of them made a profit, with the exception of one servant who decided to hide his mina in a handkerchief. Upon the nobleman's return, he chastised the slothful servant and took away his mina. The faithful servants, on the other hand, were rewarded very well.

A ruthless, violent subplot is also going on inside this parable. Besides the story of the nobleman's servants, there was the matter of his citizens—citizens who were not fond of him.

> *"But his citizens hated him, and sent a delegation after him, saying, 'We will not have this man to reign over us.' "*
> *(Luke 19:14 NASB)*

After first dealing out rewards and punishments to his servants, the nobleman focused his attention on those citizens who refused to live under his lordship.

> *"But bring here those enemies of mine, who did not want me*

to reign over them, and slay them before me."
(Luke 19:27 CSB)

In the parable, Jesus boldly warns those who refuse to accept His reign, who hate Him, who are His enemies whom He will not be trying to win over with hugs, kisses or olive branches. He will not build them a house in the hope that His generosity will convert them. He will not be offering them free food, gift baskets or—as one outreach ministry suggests—haircuts, manicures and trash cleanup to woo them.

In fact, it is not good enough for Jesus to know these rebellious servants are going to be slain. He wants to see each and every one of them slaughtered before His eyes.

Throughout the New Testament, the portrayal of Jesus is far from that of a mealy-mouthed, spineless and feeble weakling. Jesus did *not* come to bring "peace." More accurately, He came to draw dividing lines.

"Suppose ye that I am come to give peace on earth? I tell you, Nay; but rather division." (Luke 12:51)

This division will be far graver than just between neighbor and neighbor or friend and foe:

"The father shall be divided against the son, and the son against the father; the mother against the daughter, and the daughter against the mother; the mother in law against her daughter in law, and the daughter in law against her mother in law." (Luke 12:53)

For a sense of what this will be like, witness the family divisions in many Muslim countries which cause a father to put a son or daughter to death for accepting Christ.

Jesus did not vow just to bring "division" with Him. He promised fire as well.

"I have come to cast fire upon the earth; and how I wish it were already kindled!" (Luke 12:49 NASB)

Jesus: No Passive Weakling

Rather than portraying Jesus as a mild-mannered, cuddly teddy bear, the Bible depicts Him as a powerful king, a ruler unafraid to take up the sword, bind people hand and foot, cast unbelievers into outer darkness, throw them into a lake of fire, flog those who rebel, slam doors shut on sinners, slaughter enemies before His own eyes. He is described as a man who is willing to storm into a temple with a scourge of cords in His hands and overturn tables.

Twice Jesus flew into a rage against those who were converting his Father's House into a "house of merchandise," once at the beginning of His ministry and once again a few weeks before His death.

His first cleansing is recorded in the Gospel of John:

> *"When He had made a scourge of small cords, He drove them all out of the temple, and the sheep, and the oxen; and poured out the changers' money, and overthrew the tables."*
> *(John 2:15)*

His second cleansing is recorded in the Gospel of Mark:

> *"And they came to Jerusalem. And Jesus went into the temple, and began to cast out of them that sold and bought in the temple, and overthrew the tables of the moneychangers, and the seats of those who sold doves. And He would not allow anyone to carry wares through the temple." (Mark 11:15-16)*

Have you ever closed your eyes to imagine what this scene must have looked like some two millennia ago? Tables were being tossed about and thrown upside down. A scourge was in Jesus' hand as he savagely whipped and drove out moneychangers. Jesus was standing in the doorway using His body and whip to stop "anyone" from carrying merchandise through the temple. He was yelling and screaming. Animals were in a panic. Doves were flapping.

> *"For the zeal of thine house hath eaten me up; and the reproaches of them that reproached thee are fallen upon me."*
> *(Ps. 69:9)*

This is hard for many Christians to visualize, this picture of an angry Jesus, a violent Jesus, Jesus on a rampage, a Jesus who is a zealous, pitiless warrior.

After this second cleansing of the temple, the scribes and chief priests feared Him. They were astonished, and they wanted Him dead.

> *"And the scribes and chief priests heard it, and sought **how***

they might destroy him: for they feared him, because all the people was astonished at his doctrine." (Mark 11:18, emphasis added)

There are a couple of key words in this passage, in particular "feared" and "astonished."

The Greek word used for "feared" is *ephobounto*. It means "to put to flight, to terrify, frighten." The Greek word for "astonished" is *explēsseto*. It means "to strike with panic."

After Jesus' violent attack on the temple the Jewish leaders were terrified, in a state of panic, put to flight. They were so frightened that they wanted to destroy and kill Jesus.

Do God's Enemies Fear Us?

Now here's an important question: Do the enemies of God fear us? Do we terrify them? Are we putting them to flight? Are we striking them with panic?

This is what Jesus did. When he was eventually killed He died for the sins of mankind, but He was killed also because the enemies of God feared Him. They feared His message, His teachings, His mission. And after His cleansing of the temple, they feared His violence.

Let me assure you, the enemies of God will not want to kill or harm you simply because you are preaching a message of salvation. Instead, they will want you dead or silenced because you are preaching a message that is in direct contradiction to the beliefs they so energetically promote as postmodern, non-Judeo-Christian truths.

The message that Muhammad is a false prophet will get you killed in many Muslim countries.

The belief that God "created them male and female" may not get you killed, but it could get your children taken away if you live in a province in Canada. Ontario passed a law known as "The Supporting Children, Youth and Families Act of 2017" that gives the government the power to take away your child if you do not unquestioningly accept that child's chosen "gender identity" or "gender expression."

In California, the state senate passed a proposed law in 2017 that makes it a crime if you refuse to use a transgender person's preferred pronoun. In other words, if a boy wants to be known as a girl, you

The Tennes family of Michigan. "All of a sudden I felt like we couldn't even believe what we wanted to believe. We had to be quiet," said Bridget Tennes.

had better call that boy "she" or "her." Under this senate bill, anyone "willfully and repeatedly" refusing to use the preferred name or pronoun of a transgender person would not only face a $1,000 fine, but a year in jail.

Can you imagine standing in a prison holding cell, next to a murderer, and explaining that your crime was that you dared to call a biological boy a boy rather than a girl? Such a law would make a mockery out of our justice and prison systems.

We have already discussed how speaking out against gay marriage may get you fined, jailed or thrown into re-education classes.

East Lansing, Mich., will not let you sell your products at a farmer's market if you oppose gay marriage. This happened to a family who had been farming in Michigan for generations. When city officials learned that members of the family wrote a Facebook post opposing gay marriage, it refused to allow them to sell their produce—

apples, blueberries, pumpkins and sweet corn—at the town's market.

As astounding as it is that the government may take away your children because you refuse to acknowledge your child's imaginary gender change, it is equally shocking that the government can bar you from participating in local commerce because of your Christian beliefs on homosexual marriage.

The enemies of God, whom I call the "last days man," hate, despise and are repulsed at God's eternal truths. Their job is to instill fear into you, get you to change, by compulsion if necessary, and even kill you if all else fails.

But do they fear us as we try to conquer evil with love, open arms, warm embraces, kisses and pulling on heartstrings? Of course not.

A People to be Feared?

The enemies of God are completely willing to use fear to bend us to their will, desires and troublemaking. They will eventually do whatever is needed to force us into compliance. In some parts of the world, the most horrendous acts are already happening. Witness what ISIS fighters did to Christian children in Syria after first burning six Christian men who were working at a bakery.

"After that, they caught some 250 kids and kneaded them like dough in the bakery dough machine," Alice Assaf told a reporter. "They were put in the dough mixer, they were kneaded. The oldest one of them was four years old." (New York Post, Nov. 26, 2016)

That's horrible to read, but being ignorant of the insidious devices of the enemy is no more a solution to stopping the enemy than reaching out to him with open arms.

Several times the Jewish leaders tried to put fear into Christ. They tried to stone Him, throw Him off a cliff, assassinate Him. When all was said and done they feared Jesus, not the other way around. They certainly feared His message and they were terrified of Him personally.

Jewish leaders also feared the followers of Jesus. The Gospel of Mark tells this story of Herod, who wanted to put Jesus to death:

> "And when he would have put him to death, he feared the multitude, because they counted him as a prophet." (Matt. 14:5)

The term "fear" here is the same Greek word used to describe the fear Jewish leaders had of Jesus after he cleansed the temple. They were terrified, frightened, put to flight.

Herod was not worried that Jesus' followers were going to assault him with prayer, Bible verses and song. He was worried they were going to kill him.

Where are such followers of Jesus nowadays?

A similar account is given after Jesus told the Parable of the Wicked Vinedressers.

> *"And when the chief priests and Pharisees had heard his parables, they perceived that he spake of them. But when they sought to lay hands on him, **they feared the multitude**, because they took him for a prophet." (Matt. 21:45-46, emphasis added)*

Jesus's followers were willing to use violence to protect their prophet and His message.

Jewish leaders even feared the followers of John the Baptist, as told in a passage found in the Gospel of Mark:

> *"The baptism of John, was it from heaven, or of men? Answer me. And they reasoned with themselves, saying, If we shall say, From heaven; he will say, Why then did ye not believe him? But we shall say, Of men; **they feared the people:** for all men counted John, that he was a prophet indeed." (Mark 11:30-32, emphasis added)*

According to the Roman historian Josephus, one of the reasons Herod Antipas had John the Baptist beheaded was over his fear that John's followers would commit sedition.

"Herod became alarmed," Josephus wrote, because Herod feared that John's followers "might lead to some form of sedition, for it looked as if they would be guided by John in everything that they did."

> *"Herod decided therefore that it would be much better to strike first and be rid of him before his work **led to an uprising**, than to wait for an **upheaval**, get involved in a difficult situation and see his mistake." (Antiquities 18.116-119, emphasis added)*

There is absolutely no record, either in the Bible or any other historical writing, that John or Jesus attempted to present their followers as people who should not be feared. Even up to the point of Jesus' death, Jewish leaders feared His followers.

> *"Now the feast of unleavened bread drew nigh, which is*
> *called the Passover. And the chief priests and scribes sought*
> *how they might kill him; **for they feared the people**."*
> *(Luke 22:1-2, emphasis added)*

Jewish leaders so feared the followers of Jesus that they had to arrest him in the dark of night, out of sight of the multitude and (this is important) in the company of Roman soldiers. The point being, Jewish leaders feared the followers of Jesus so much that they felt safe only if they had Roman soldiers around to keep order and protect them.

Upon His arrest Jesus even mocked their fear of His followers with a rhetorical statement:

> *"When I was daily with you in the temple, ye stretched forth*
> *no hands against me: but this is your hour, and the power of*
> *darkness." (Luke 22:53)*

Jesus and the Jewish leaders knew exactly what would have happened if they had "stretched forth" their hands against Him in broad daylight, in the open court of the temple and in front of his loyal followers.

So the Sanhedrin hatched a plan to arrest Jesus at night in the Garden of Gethsemane. Even this was risky and the religious leaders felt safe only if they were escorted by Roman guards.

Not surprisingly (and as the Jewish leaders had rightly anticipated) one of them was attacked. Peter drew a sword and cut off the ear of the high priest's servant. Jesus immediately healed the ear and told Peter to put his sword back in its sheath, saying, "For all they that take the sword shall perish with the sword." (Matt. 26:52)

Jesus' statement, of course, was figurative rather than literal. Obviously not everyone who takes up a sword also is killed by one. By no means, then, was Jesus reprimanding Peter for having a sword. In fact, Jesus encouraged it.

Take up the Sword

As Jesus prepared His disciples before His death, He told them:

> " 'When I sent you without purse, and scrip, and shoes, lacked
> ye any thing?' And they said, Nothing. Then said he unto
> them, 'But now, he that hath a purse, let him take it, and like-
> wise his scrip: **and he that hath no sword**, let him sell his
> garment, and **buy one.**' " (Luke 22:35-36, emphasis added)

How important is it for Christians to have a sword? Jesus said that
if you don't have a sword, dig deep into your purse and pull out
coinage or scrip (paper money) and buy one. If there still aren't
enough funds, then sell your garments. But get one.

The disciples didn't hesitate in their response. They did not ask
why. They did not question Him about His previous comments on
turning the other cheek, or loving your enemies or praying for those
who hate you. They did not remind Him that he once said, "bless
those who mistreat you;" or His command that "ye not resist evil;" or
that He also said, "Blessed are the peacemakers."

Rather, they said just the opposite.

> "And they said, 'Lord, behold, here are two swords.' And he
> said unto them, 'It is enough.' " (Luke 22:38)

It is interesting, sad and humorous to see how so many Bible commentators and scholars twist themselves into knots to make this passage go away.

Some claim the word "sword" is just a figure of speech, an allegory that should not be taken literally. Some say the word should
never have been included in the verse. One commentator suggested
Jesus was simply preparing his disciples to defend themselves against
the wild beasts of the wilderness after they fled.

Others even claim Jesus was merely telling his disciples to buy a
knife to use as an eating utensil.

Here are a few examples of Bible commentators trying to white-
wash Jesus's command to buy a sword: "It must evidently be taken
figuratively," says James Nisbet. "The country was infested with rob-
bers and wild beasts," says Albert Barnes, explaining the need for
swords. John Gill cautions, "These words of Christ are not to be understood literally." The *Geneva Study Bible* says, "He says all this using
an allegory." *Wesley's Explanatory Notes* says, "It is plain, this is not be
taken literally."

Not all Bible commentators are so dismissive of Jesus's clear, articulate and unequivocal command to acquire a sword, even if you have to sell your clothes to do so.

The Expositor's Greek Testament says, "A sword is the one thing that is needful. This is a realistic speech true to the manner of Jesus and, what is rare in Luke, given without toning down, a genuine logion *(a saying attributed to Jesus)* without a doubt."

Bible commentator James Burton Coffman was probably the best at defending the literal translation of these verses. It is worth taking the time to read it:

> *"The absolute pacifist tradition among Christians of all ages and the acceptance of it by many commentators make this verse 'a real problem' for many. Most commentators view the passage as figurative, as did [Norval] Geldenhuys, who said, 'The Lord intended (these words) in a figurative sense.' But if the sword is figurative, what about the purse, the wallet, and the cloak?*

> *"As [Herschel] Hobbs said, 'It is impossible to tone down this statement; neither can we dismiss it as not being a genuine saying of Jesus.' The clear meaning of the passage is that 'a sword' is the one thing needful, even surpassing in priority such an important item as a cloak. The two errors to be avoided here are (1) the supposition that the gospel should be spread by the sword, and (2) the notion that a sword should ever be employed against lawful authority. Before the evening was over, the Lord would have further occasion to demonstrate the proper and improper uses of the sword. Barnes was certainly correct in his view that 'These directions (concerning the sword) were not made with reference to his being taken in the garden but to their future lives.'*

> *"... the view maintained here is that self-defense is exactly what Jesus taught. Self-defense is a basic, natural right of all men, and there is no lawful government on earth that denies it. Just why should it be supposed that Jesus denied to Christians such a basic right has never been explained.*

*'Resist not evil ... go the second mile ... turn the other
cheek... give thy cloak also, etc.' are not applicable to situations in which one's life is threatened, or endangered."*

Not Merely for Self-Defense

Although Coffman emphasizes the need for a sword to provide
self-defense, positioning it as a basic human right against all forms of
aggressors (including governments), it is clear Jesus was asking His
disciples to bear a sword for something much deeper, more profound
and markedly expansive than simple self-defense.

Christians will need a sword to defend themselves against the enemies of God—who are not necessarily there to rob or rape.

The literal interpretation of this piece of scripture expresses ur-
gency. Danger is coming, and its coming is a certainty. It is so certain
that if you do not have the money to buy a weapon, you need to come
up with it. Sell the clothes off your back if you have to.

This does not sound like a warning from Jesus over a hypothetical
robber who may or may not ever attack you. No one would ever take
every dime they had to buy a weapon, even forfeiting their own clothing, for protection against the mere possibility of thuggery. No. They
would do what most people would in that situation: buy one when
they could comfortably afford it.

It is not just your physical body that Christ wants you to protect; it
is much more than that. Similarly to Christ violently protecting His
Father's Temple, He wants you to protect your own temple, for you
"are being built up as a spiritual house for a holy priesthood ... "(1
Peter 2:5)

> *"Know ye not that ye are the temple of God, and that the
> Spirit of God dwelleth in you? If any man defile the temple of
> God, him shall God destroy; for the temple of God is holy,
> which temple ye are." (1 Cor. 3:16-17)*

Some—actually many—have interpreted this verse as a condemnation of suicide. But it is clear the verse means a Christian has the
right to protect and defend his temple of God. You have an absolute
right to protect that temple just as Jesus defended His father's temple.
It houses the Spirit of God. It should never be defiled or destroyed by

others, and those who try to defile it should be destroyed.

To be clearer, you have the right to protect yourself against anyone who would force you to violate the Word of God.

A Duty to God and Oneself

In May of 2017, a group of Muslims in military fatigues waved down a bus filled with Christians in Cairo. It appeared they were stopping the bus for military reasons, but they weren't. They weren't even real military. They were radical Islamists. They had no plans to rob the passengers or rape the women. They had no interest in taking hostages or hijacking the bus. Their only interest was converting the Christians to Islam.

As one passenger related his experience to *The New York Times*, "They told the men to recite the *shahada,* the Islamic declaration of faith. When the men refused, the gunmen opened fire."

"We told them that we are Christians and we will die Christians," Samia Adly told the *Washington Post.*

Die they did. Thirty were executed. Twenty-six were wounded. None had a weapon, but they were all wearing clothes. Had they sold their garments to buy a sword they might be unharmed today. Instead they were defenseless to protect the temple of God and the Spirit of God that dwells in them. This is not meant to diminish in any way the great sacrifice they made or the courage they displayed. But this is precisely why Jesus told Christians to "get a sword."

It does not matter whether it is legal or illegal to have or carry a weapon in your state, according to the teachings of Jesus. During His time in Jerusalem it was illegal for citizens to carry swords, yet Jesus told His disciples to arm themselves. When the disciples found two, he said it was enough. When Peter cut off the ear of the high priest's servant, Jesus did not tell him to throw away the sword. Neither did he lecture about obeying the law. Instead he told Peter, "Put thy sword into the sheath." (John 18:11)

It is your duty to defend the temple of God, your body, against all who would attempt to steal and violate God's eternal truths, which it houses.

"But know this, that if the goodman of the house had known

in what watch the thief would come, he would have watched,
and would not have suffered his house to be broken up."
(Matt. 24:43)

The "goodman" of course would have protected his house with more than just a watchful eye. That thief would have been met with a sword.

The threat of Christian violence can also be found in the writings of the early church, as was recorded in the *Acts of the Apostles.*

Luke tells the story of the Apostles, arrested and thrown into prison one day, who were miraculously found the following day preaching the gospel in the temple. "Look," someone said, "the men whom you put in prison are standing in the temple teaching the people!" The captain of the temple guards, fearing the multitude might kill him and his crew, made sure the Apostles were arrested without using force.

"Then went the captain with the officers, and brought them
without violence: **for they feared the people, lest they**
should have been stoned." *(Acts 5:26, emphasis added)*

As shown in this chapter, there are many instances in the New Testament where the threat of retaliatory violence is portrayed as an effective way to counter violent enemies.

CHAPTER FOUR:

ARE WE WORTH OUR SALT?

There are many places on Earth where being a Christian is the most dangerous thing you can be.

(Robert Nicholson of the Philos Project)

Christianity is under attack from all sides, on every front, from every angle and all around the globe.

If radical Islamists have anything to do with it, things are not going to get better.

"What is coming is tougher and worse for the worshippers of the Cross and their helpers, Allah permitting," read one official statement from ISIS in May 2017.

It was shortly after this statement that ISIS wreaked its carnage on a busload of Christians in Cairo, Egypt, as recounted in the previous chapter. A few days later, ISIS followers slaughtered eight people in the Philippines simply because they refused to accept the *shahada,* the Muslim proclamation of faith.

An ISIS member followed up deadly terrorist attacks in London, England in 2017 with this message, posted on the Internet:

> *"You now see your days turning dark and full of fear and terror. You can expect the future to be darker still, with Allah's help ... Rest assured that, just as you burn our children, we will light a fire under your feet and roast your rotten flesh, with the help of Allah the Almighty."*

"So expect worse to come," the ISIS supporter said. "We shall fill your hearts with fear and terror by means of ramming attacks and beheadings."

Expect worse to come? That's a chilling statement considering what ISIS had already done to Syrian Christians in the fall of 2016.

ISIS: "Expect worse to come ... we shall fill your hearts with fear and terror."

ness of this world, against spiritual wickedness in high
places." (Eph. 6:12)

That wrestling (also described as a battle, fight and war in other Bible editions) is most often preached as a struggle against personal sin. That is an incomplete—if not completely wrong—reading of that passage.

The Bible, in many places, tells us to strive and resist against sin, such as in Heb. 12:4: "Ye have not yet resisted unto blood, striving against sin."

But the Apostle Paul in Ephesians 6:12 is not talking about wrestling against personal sin. He is talking about resisting an outward evil, which he explains in the next verse.

"Therefore, take up the full armor of God, so that you will be
able to **resist in the evil day**, and having done everything,
to stand firm." (Eph. 6:13, NASB, emphasis added)

The 'Evil Day' Ahead

The "evil day" is not a reference to personal sin. It is external to one's inner self, a malignant wickedness that demands for one to do everything to resist and stand firm. The word "resist" means "stand against" in Greek. It is not a passive concept, but means to take an active stand against an evil person or people.

As theologian Adam Clarke commented: "Maintain your ground against them, never putting off your armor, but standing always ready prepared to repel any new attack."

Theologian Jon Gill says it means to "face him, and give him battle." John Calvin says it means to "fight valiantly to the end."

Theologian James Nisbet interprets the verse this way: "A sloucher cannot fight. And it is the end. It is comparatively easy to drive back an enemy in the first rush; but the crucial test comes when soldiers are required to stand firm, and to hold their ground against an ever-returning, ever-increasing foe."

"Resist in the evil day" does not mean run and hide, ignore and keep silent, or compromise and negotiate.

There's no question that a ghastly "evil day" unfolded for the Egyptian Christians traveling in the Cairo bus when they were boarded and compelled either to accept the Muslim faith or take a bullet to the head. Praise and honor can only be afforded to the thirty souls who died and the twenty-six who were wounded. It is evident that each had a breastplate of righteousness and a shield of faith. On each head was a helmet of salvation and in their hearts was the sword of the Spirit.

They lacked one important thing: physical swords in their hands.

It was precisely for incidents such as this that Jesus said, "He that hath no sword, let him sell his garment, and buy one."

Anyone watching the news knows more "evil days" are coming for Christians. As far back as 2012, German Chancellor Angela Merkel saw it and said, "Christianity is the most persecuted religion in the world."

The *Center for Studies on New Religions* reported that in 2016 alone 90,000 Christians were murdered.

U.S. Vice President Mike Pence, speaking at the first World Summit in Defense of Persecuted Christians, said the "Christian faith is under siege" and that "no people of faith today face greater hostility and hatred than followers of Christ."

Christian persecution in the Middle East, the birthplace of Christianity, is so brutal that in 2015 the *New York Times* ran the headline, "Is This the End of Christianity in the Middle East?"

What a frightening and poignant question to ask.

The Actual Meaning of Persecution

The current scourging of Christianity in the Middle East can of course be laid at the feet of Islamic extremism, ISIS being the most notable culprit. Writing for CNN in November of 2016, journalist Moni Basu paints a black image for the survival of Christianity in the Middle East: "Christianity came early but is now edging dangerously close to extinction."

Christians in Iraq have responded by forming their own militia to battle ISIS forces. As of 2016, they boasted a 100,000-man Christian army called the Babylon Brigade. Iraqi Christians had finally become fed up with their homes being stolen, businesses snatched, family members beheaded or blown apart, wives raped, and their children kidnapped, sold as slaves or forced to accept Islam or die. They were also tired of watching ISIS destroy Christian artifacts, monuments and monasteries.

The overarching goal of ISIS is not only to kill Christians, but also to erase all signs of Christianity—buildings, icons, books, relics, art.

U.S. Marine Colonel Matthew Bogdanos, an assistant district attorney for Manhattan, explained it: "Once you destroy the cultural

Bradley Manning ... Chelsea Manning. Sex reassignment surgery provided at taxpayer expense.

heritage of a people, you are in effect attacking and destroying their cultural identity. Once you destroy their cultural identity, it's but a short step to destroy and eradicate the people themselves."

It is easy when we hear or see the word *persecution* to conjure up images of imprisonments, beheadings, starvations, dismemberments and torture—all of which have been directed against Christians at some point in history. But these tragedies often represent only the final stage of a society's persecution. The confiscation of scripture, the burning of churches, the refusal to allow Christians to serve in public office and the outlawing of Christianity itself have served as precursors to harsher forms of punishment dating back to the days of the Roman Emperor Diocletian, the years 284 to 305.

In a more liberal western society such as the United States, these milder forms of persecution are actually a necessary step before more extreme ones can take hold, such as throwing Christians in jail or harming them physically.

To be clear, persecution does not always have to be at the hands of the state. Individuals, activists, the media, corporations, organizations and other religions can persecute Christians and often do.

We must not be trapped into a myopic, personal view of persecution. When Christ said, "If they persecuted me, they will also persecute you" (John 15:20), certainly He was talking about you as a Christian individual. He was also talking, however, about the manifestations of Christianity. Your beliefs, traditions and practices as a Christian can be persecuted just as ruthlessly as can be your physical body.

In May 2017, the U.S. Department of Health and Human Services made a ruling that all hospitals, including religious hospitals, must perform abortions and "sex reassignment" surgeries even if doing so would violate the religious beliefs of the institution or its employees. Failure to perform abortions or sex reassignments would result in forfeiture of federal funds by the religious hospitals.

This is nothing less than direct persecution of the Christian faith. It may be considered only a "mild" persecution because failure to comply results in loss of funds and institutional tax benefits, but it could also mean employment termination for doctors, nurses and other medical staff who refuse to perform the unchristian procedures

According to Strong's *Dictionary,* the word "persecute" in John 15:20 means, "in any way whatever to harass, trouble, molest." As Christian warriors, of course, we should refuse to meekly submit to laws, ordinances or edicts that force us to violate the Word of God. In fact, we are instructed to do the opposite. Jude tells us to "contend for the faith." (Jude 1:3)

The Apostle Paul says, "I am set for the defense of the gospel." (Phil. 1:17) He adds, "We are destroying speculations and every lofty thing raised up against the knowledge of God." (2 Cor. 10:5)

The notion that an unborn baby is not a human being and can therefore be killed by a doctor or mother is "a lofty thing" that needs destroying. The same can be said regarding the lofty speculations of gender fluidity and homosexual "marriage."

Most everyone is familiar with Peter and the response of other apostles when they were commanded to stop teaching in the name of Christ: "We ought to obey God rather than men." (Acts 5:29)

Not only are Christians expected to disobey laws that are contrary to the Gospel, but they are also to actively contend with and destroy these arguments, be they laws or speculations.

A Duty to Resist

Torture, imprisonment and martyrdom are only the most extreme manifestations of persecution. Persecution can also be subtle, like forcing people to violate their Christian beliefs.

That happened to Jack Phillips, owner of the Masterpiece Cakeshop in Lakewood, Colo. After his shop refused to prepare a wedding cake to be used in a homosexual wedding, the state ordered him to make gay wedding cakes in the future and also required him—along with his staff—to attend sensitivity training classes where their beliefs could presumably be attacked and reshaped.

This is persecution, as his attorney, Nicolle Martin, aptly pointed out to Fox News:

"They are turning people of faith into religious refugees. Is this the society that we want to live in, where people of faith are driven out of business?" Martin asked reporter and political commentator Todd Starnes.

The attack on Mr. Phillips' faith went beyond just ordering him to perform an act that violates his Christian faith. By forcing him and his staff into sensitivity training classes, the state was attempting to force them to change their Christian beliefs, alter their very way of thinking.

"My 87-year-old mom works here and she says she's not being rehabilitated," Phillips responded to the state order.

Persecution Here and Now, in the Western World

In 2015 a county clerk in Kentucky, Kim Davis, went to jail rather than issue a marriage license to a homosexual couple. To grant the license, she believed, would have violated her Christian beliefs. In Tampa, Fla. a high school teacher told her students they were forbidden to wear the Christian cross in her classroom. In Louisburg, Kan., police told a woman she wasn't even allowed to pray in her own home.

Cases such as these are far too numerous to all be listed here. All qualify as persecution. Stripping people of the right to show and act lawfully upon their Christian beliefs is a precursor to more serious and frightening forms of persecution.

As an example, let's bring our attention once again to the Ontario, Canada law passed in 2017 that prevents parents from rejecting their child's chosen "gender identity."

The Ontario government considers it a "form of abuse, when a child identifies one way and a caregiver is saying no, you need to do this differently," explained Minister of Children and Youth Services Michael Coteau.

Coteau told Breitbart News, "If it's abuse, and if it's within the definition, a child can be removed from that environment and placed into protection where the abuse stops."

What are Christian parents to do in such a situation, in which they are clearly being persecuted over their faith? Should they reject biblical doctrine? Should they remain faithful to the Bible and allow the state to snatch their children from under their care and roof? Should they move to a different country?

This kind of persecution is even harsher than going to jail, paying fines or attending sensitivity classes. This is invading your family, ripping your child from your arms because your Christian beliefs are considered child abuse.

How are the effects of this law any different than a complete stranger entering your home and snatching your child? At least a stranger is not so brazen as to walk into your home and take your child in broad daylight, turning the law itself against you. Do we make an exception when the state passes a law allowing a different type of stranger—one with a badge, a gun and a court order—to enter you home and seize your child?

Stealing Our Children to 'Protect' Them

Most Christians think persecution will simply be a matter of opposition to their personal faith in Jesus Christ. In the Muslim world that may very well be the case; ex-Muslims have routinely been killed for converting to Christianity. In the secular world, however, persecution is not likely to occur over a profession of Christianity, but rather over the eternal truths that Christianity represents. (Though this is beginning to change with rising violence against congregants inside their churches.)

In Norway, Marius and Ruth Bodnariu lost four of their children to the state—two sons and two daughters—after authorities accused them of being "radical Christians who were indoctrinating their children." It took nearly a year and a half for the state to return their children, and even then it was only because of international outrage.

Norway? Canada? Why should Christians in America be concerned? The obvious answer is that the Kingdom of God has no borders. A wall, a river, a guardhouse or an ocean never separates Christians from their brothers and sisters. Also, social ills elsewhere in the West always seep into the United States. A poll reported in the *Daily Wire* in 2017 found that nearly half of U.S. millennials are open to the idea of government removing children from homes if parents refuse to accept their child's transgender transitioning. The seeping is well under way.

Most assuredly, there will soon be a crazy city or town in America that will pass legislation mirroring the Ontario law demanding similar removal of children, much in the same manner that the state of Oregon passed a law allowing citizens to claim "non-binary" as their gender on their driver's licenses. Within weeks the city of Washington, D.C., our nation's capital, passed similar legislation allowing drivers to choose "X" as a "gender neutral" option for their license to drive.

In Delaware, the state Department of Education proposed new school guidelines that would allow children to change both their gender *and* their race (Regulation 225, Prohibition of Discrimination), science be damned. Since the child can do this without mom or dad even knowing, then parents be damned as well. Will it soon be regarded as child abuse to tell your Caucasian boy that he is really not an African-American girl?

So What Are We to Do?

Hearing, helping and defending Christians, no matter where they live, is an obligation of our faith. The Bible tells us *we are God's army*, we are the salt of the Earth, a light to the world and a city set upon a hill.

In all these expressions the symbolism is obvious: Christians have a duty, a responsibility, a mission to defend and present God's truth to the world regardless of consequences.

Furthermore, these expressions are not just meant for a congregation occupying a church building. They are meant for individual Christians wherever they live, work or roam:

> " 'What I tell you in the darkness, speak in the light; and what you hear whispered in your ear, proclaim upon the housetops,' Jesus said." (Matt. 10:27 NASB)

This is more than passive resistance to ungodly laws; it is actively defending and presenting God's truths. Failure to do so will eventually allow "mild" persecution (such as losing your job or tax benefits) to turn into something unimaginably horrific.

Evangelism and spreading the Gospel is more than offering people a plan for salvation. They must first know they are fallen. They must know God's truths. They must know the consequences of sin.

God sent the Holy Spirit for this very purpose.

> "I will send Him to you. And He, when He comes, will con-

vict the world concerning sin and righteousness and judg-
ment." (John 16:7-8 NASB)

The Holy Spirit does this through you, not on His own.

When people come to Christ they gain more than eternal salvation in the afterlife. They gain salvation from personal destruction in their present life. They are being rescued from God's wrath in the "here and now."

If someone is a drug addict, we want to rescue him from his addiction even if he rejects Christ. We want people to understand the truths of God regardless of whether they eventually accept Christ as their Lord and Savior.

"Thou shalt not steal"? That is a truth from God that needs to apply to all humanity, not just Christians. The same can be said for other biblical instructions against bribery, bearing false witness, cheating, murder, rape, etc.

We Are Supposed to Be the Salt of the Earth

As a city set on a hill, and a light to the world, we bear testimony of God's truths to a godless world irrespective of personal opinions, religious beliefs or laws. We are the salt of the Earth, meaning we are not only here to give flavor to the world, but to act as a preserver of God's glorious truths. If we fail to do this, we are worthless as a Christian body.

"You are the salt of the earth; but if the salt has become taste-
less, how can it be made salty again? It is no longer good for
anything, except to be thrown out and trampled under foot
by men." (Matt. 5:13 NASB)

That's exactly what *will* happen if the Christian body loses its "saltiness." We will be thrown out and trampled upon like dirt.

That trampling—that casting aside—can be felt now.

As a result of decades of inactivity among a vast majority of churches, pastors and Christians, America is now steeped in a social and moral crisis from which many believe she may never recover.

We now live in country where elite educators, those who instruct and teach our children, deny loudly that there is a difference between male and female. They claim children can be "gender-neutral," choosing which sex they want to be, or even inventing a new one.

Such fanciful absurdity was foretold by Paul when he said, "They exchanged the truth of God for a lie." (Romans 1:25 NASB)

No wonder these people can't see God; they can't even look at a human body and determine whether to call it male or female. Unfortunately, however, in America we are losing the battle over so-called "gender neutrality."

It all begs an important question: How did Christians in America become so un-salty and tasteless that we are actually losing the battle on whether to call a child a boy or a girl? How are we losing such a basic, common sense, scientific, grade-school argument?

Without the truth of God being pressed and pushed on an unbelieving world, depravity will result, as the Apostle Paul also foretold:

> *"And just as they did not see fit to acknowledge God any*
> *longer, God gave them over to a depraved mind, to do those*
> *things which are not proper." (Rom. 1:28 NASB)*

Not surprising. Christians are not taught these days to be warriors for God's eternal truths.

> *"You have made them to be a kingdom and priests to our*
> *God; and they will reign upon the earth." (Rev. 5:10 NASB)*

How many churches actually tell their congregations this, that God has made them kings and priests to reign on Earth? We are kings and priests *now*, not in some far-off, distant, after-death future. The Kingdom of Christ is already here. Our mission is to cast Satan out of this world.

> *"Now judgment is upon this world; now the ruler of this*
> *world will be cast out." (John 12:31 NASB)*

Our job is to bring that Kingdom, in all its glory, to victory over Satan. When we do, the end will come and Jesus will deliver that Kingdom over to God, His Father.

> *"Then cometh the end, when he shall have delivered up the*
> *kingdom to God, even the Father; when he shall have put*
> *down all rule and all authority and power." (1 Cor. 15:24)*

CHAPTER FIVE:

GETTING TO KNOW THE ENEMY

From the days of John the Baptist until now
the kingdom of heaven suffers violence,
and violent men take it by force.
(Matt. 11:12 NASB)

Oh, these uncomfortable scriptures—verses that few pastors want to talk about, much less spend an entire Sunday service explaining. We already discussed a few of these difficult verses: Jesus coming to bring division upon the Earth, with a sword and no peace. Jesus telling His disciples to pick up a sword. Jesus saying He came to bring fire upon the Earth, wishing it was already kindled. Jesus entering the temple, overturning tables and using a whip of cords to chase out the moneychangers.

Now for another verse that is rarely addressed, the one just above at the start of the chapter: "The kingdom of heaven suffers violence and violent men take it by force."

This should not surprise us. Never in the experience of mankind has a kingdom existed that has avoided violence. Why should the kingdom of God be any different?

Like earthly kingdoms, the kingdom of God has treasures that others find valuable. "The kingdom of heaven is like a treasure hidden in the field," says Jesus. (Matt 13:44 NASB)

Enemies of God's kingdom would like to occupy it, strip it of its treasures or at the very least render it ineffective if it can't be dismantled or demolished.

The job of the Christian warrior is to protect God's kingdom and destroy its enemies. To be clear, to protect and destroy does not necessarily mean to physically kill the enemy, though this may be necessary. That will be discussed in the next chapter.

Also, like earthly kingdoms, the kingdom of God has ambassadors. The role of ambassador is to reconcile people to God:

> *"Therefore, we are ambassadors for Christ ... we beg you on behalf of Christ, be reconciled to God." (2 Cor. 5:20 NASB)*

The heavenly kingdom has soldiers. The duty of the soldier is to engage in war and never get distracted with worldly affairs.

> *"No man that warreth entangleth himself with the affairs of this life; that he may please him who hath chosen him to be a soldier." (2 Tim 2:4)*

The kingdom of God has power.

> *"For the kingdom of God is not in word, but in power." (1 Cor. 4:20)*

That power is tremendous, with the ability to thwart evil on Earth and release what is good.

> *"... whatsoever thou shalt bind on earth shall be bound in heaven: and whatsoever thou shalt loose on earth shall be loosed in heaven." (Matt. 16:19)*

Of course the kingdom has a king, that king being Jesus Christ:

> *"And on His robe and on His thigh He has a name written, 'KING OF KINGS, AND LORD OF LORDS.' " (Rev. 19:16 NASB)*

Our Mission: The Kingdom of God

How important is the kingdom of God for Christians? It is so important that it is the reason Jesus came to Earth. Contrary to popular Christian belief, and the message of so many churches nowadays, Jesus did not come for the purpose of preaching, spreading or offering love.

Jesus did not come to smile and be some sort of Wal-Mart greeter. The purpose of Jesus was to preach the kingdom of God:

> *"But He said to them, 'I must preach the kingdom of God to the other cities also, for I was sent for this purpose.' " (Luke 4:43 NASB)*

Jesus sent His disciples not with the mission of spreading His love, but with the task of preaching the kingdom of God.

"And he sent them to preach the kingdom of God, and to heal the sick." (Luke 9:2)

When Jesus was approached by "someone" wanting to follow Him, but first wanting to bury his dead father, he did not bestow hugs, kisses, condolences and free passes. Instead:

"Jesus said unto him, Let the dead bury their dead: but go thou and preach the kingdom of God." (Luke 9:20)

What we should gather from scripture is that the kingdom of God is what Christians should be preaching. As such we should preach the totality of the kingdom.

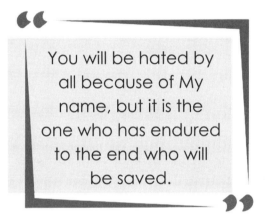

You will be hated by all because of My name, but it is the one who has endured to the end who will be saved.

If Christians simply preach the love of Christ, then why would the kingdom of God ever suffer violence? Who wants to attack love?

Jesus was very direct about the mission of the kingdom of God:

"Verily I say unto you, Whatsoever ye shall bind on earth shall be bound in heaven: and whatsoever ye shall loose on earth shall be loosed in heaven." (Matt. 18:18)

The mission of the kingdom is to both bind and turn loose. When we see evil, we bind it. When we see the truth of God, we turn it loose. But be careful: Jesus said "whatsoever" you bind and loose will also be bound and loosed in heaven. That means both good and evil.

This is what Jesus was speaking about when He said we were given "the keys to the kingdom." (Matt. 16:19)

How do we bind? We bind through prayer, through actions, through words, through power and strength. The angels in heaven are working alongside us. They are also binding in heaven, fighting satanic forces and waging war against evil. They are working to bind in heaven what we are binding on Earth. They do not work *in spite* of us. They are working *because* of us.

"For we wrestle not against flesh and blood, but against principalities, against powers, against the rulers of the darkness of this world, against spiritual wickedness in high places." (Eph. 6:12)

If we are not binding evil on Earth, then we are setting evil loose in the heavens. This is tantamount to the powers in heaven saying, "If they don't care, then we don't care." More accurately, it is like saying, "If Christians on Earth don't want to fight evil on Earth, then we are powerless to do so in heaven."

It is our job to bind. It is our mission. Jesus gave us that power.

Of course the kingdom is more than binding and setting loose, as the Apostle Paul makes clear:

"For the kingdom of God is ... righteousness, and peace, and joy in the Holy Ghost." (Rom. 14:17)

In other words, the kingdom of God is not just physical rewards, but glorious spiritual rewards as well.

The Lost Souls

These splendid rewards, however, are reserved for those who enter legitimately. Only dwellers in the kingdom receive the benefits of joy, peace, patience, gentleness, goodness, faith and love, not those who are languishing in utter hopelessness outside the kingdom's walls.

Lost souls live under the fixed condemnation of "darkness and the shadow of death" (Luke 1:79). Christ offers them a chance at redemption, of course, but it is only after they are saved that they can receive the benefits of His love.

It is important to understand this correctly. Obviously, God loves sinners. He sent his only begotten Son into the world so that "whosoever believeth in him should not perish, but have everlasting life." (John 3:16)

Yet until they are saved, the nonbelieving are like prisoners locked behind iron bars, cut off from the world, especially from their loved ones. Until they are set free they cannot enjoy the pleasures of those who want to offer them love. In the same way, the unsaved are denied the power of Christ's love—His peace, goodness, hope, spiritual healing and happiness—because they live as condemned men and women, set apart from Christ. They "are under the curse." (Gal. 3:10)

That curse must first be removed, through redemption, before they can receive the many blessed offerings of Christ's love. To accomplish this, they must understand they are sinners "and come short of the glory of God." (Rom. 3:23)

They "come short" because they do not have faith in Jesus Christ and, as such, live under the penalties of God's law.

> "But before faith came, we were kept under the law ..."
> (Gal. 3:23)

Jesus never intended for the world to love us. If we are preaching the kingdom of God correctly (and not positioning Christ as some sort of loveable, huggable Barney the purple dinosaur) then the world will indeed hate us.

> "You will be hated by all because of My name, but it is the one who has endured to the end who will be saved." (Matt. 10:22 NASB)

Not loved. Hated.

The mission of preaching the kingdom of God is to present God's law to the unbelieving, so that every man and woman knows why they fall short of His glory. They must first understand "the law" before they can understand why they need to be redeemed. Such preaching, however, can generate anger, resentment, bitterness and hostility towards the messenger. The nonbelieving do not want to be told they are sinners, that they need to repent, that they need to accept Jesus Christ as their Savior or else face condemnation for all of eternity.

Our mission is to preach whatever Christ is whispering in our ears, whatever He is telling us in the dark. Doing so will cause these enemies of God to want to kill us.

> "What I tell you in darkness, that speak ye in light: and what ye hear in the ear, that preach ye upon the housetops. And fear not them which kill the body, but are not able to kill the soul: but rather fear him which is able to destroy both soul and body in hell." (Matt. 10:27-28)

Not surprisingly, some of these lost souls want to lash out and stop such preaching. They want to silence God's message and will do whatever they can to destroy it.

Let's call them "enemies of God."

No Mercy for Sworn Enemies

There is a distinction between those who have yet to become believers in Jesus Christ and those who are flat-out enemies of God. In some aspects they are the same. For instance, both live as condemned men and women, separated from Christ.

But the enemies of God are uniquely distinct from those who are simply unsaved. They are more than just sinners leading a sinful life. The enemies of God are those who plot and vigorously pursue the destruction of God's word, His kingdom and His saints. It is with great difficulty that these people are ever saved. They are hell-bent (quite literally) on conquering God's kingdom through any means necessary—deception, infiltration or violence. They have little hope of salvation because Jesus does not want them to have salvation.

An analogy might make this distinction clearer. In any given war there are soldiers and citizens that constitute a nation. The citizens do not actively fight in the war, but mostly go about their daily business of raising families, going to work, enjoying recreation and trying to be productive. They are loyal citizens of their country and are most likely devoted to their nation's beliefs, heritage and cause, but they are not the ones carrying guns or dropping bombs.

In a war, it is typically not the goal of the opposing side to kill the citizens, but rather to "free" them from their doctrines, beliefs and government. Citizens are noncombatants who need to be saved and brought under new control.

Soldiers, however, are different. They are killers who face down their enemies. Their desire is to conquer an opponent, and they will use every strategy, tactic and weapon in their arsenal to destroy the opposing nation with the hope of imposing their own beliefs, dictums and laws on the conquered.

The same applies to the Kingdom of God. The world has sinners who want to live their lives apart from Jesus Christ, going about their daily business free from what they believe are biblical constrictions. But the world also has enemies—enemy soldiers—who want nothing more than to destroy God's kingdom.

Which leads to another uncomfortable scripture. It is the passage where Jesus tells his disciples that He speaks in parables to prevent certain nonbelievers from ever being converted:

> *"He answered and said unto them, 'Because it is given unto you to know the mysteries of the kingdom of heaven, but to them it is not given ... Therefore speak I to them in parables: because they seeing see not; and hearing they hear not, neither do they understand ... lest at any time they should see with their eyes, and hear with their ears, and should understand with their heart, **and should be converted, and I should heal them.'** " (Matt. 13:11,13,15, emphasis added)*

These souls, virtually condemned for all eternity, were created for the purpose of dishonor and destruction, as the Apostle Paul wrote to the church in Rome.

> *"What if God, willing to shew his wrath, and to make his power known, endured with much longsuffering the vessels of wrath fitted to destruction ..." (Rom. 9:22)*

King David said as much in Ps. 58:3-5 NIV:

> *"Even from birth the wicked go astray; from the womb they are wayward, spreading lies. Their venom is like the venom of a snake, like that of a cobra that has stopped its ears, that will not heed the tune of the charmer, however skillful the enchanter may be." (Ps. 58:3-5 NIV)*

It is clear there is little chance of saving these sworn enemies of God, no matter how charming or skillful the "charmer" (evangelist) may be. Their ears have been stopped. They are poisonous like snakes. They live solely to spread lies. The torture of their lives begins at birth. Yet they consider themselves shrewd and intelligent.

Jesus thanks God that the truth of salvation is hidden from them:

> *"... I thank thee, O Father, Lord of heaven and earth, because thou hast hid these things from the wise and prudent, and hast revealed them unto babes." (Matt. 11:25)*

As difficult as it may be for us mortals to understand, Jesus said He will not even pray for these people.

> *"I am not praying for the world, but for those you have given*
> *me, for they are yours." (John 17:9 NIV)*

We preach to them of course. We try to convert them of course. It is our obligation to offer them salvation. Jesus has invited all to become believers in Christ (even those He has blinded). Remember, Jesus did not say these souls can never be saved, only that it is with great difficulty because of their blindness and hardened hearts. It remains painfully obvious, however, that Christ would prefer them not to be converted, however uncomfortable that may make us feel.

Second, we preach to them because we do not know whom God has destined for destruction. We are denied such intimate knowledge; much in the same way we are denied knowledge of when we may be entertaining angels:

> *"Be not forgetful to entertain strangers: for thereby some*
> *have entertained angels unawares." (Heb. 13:2)*

The Bible calls these enemies who are destined for destruction, "serpents," "scorpions," "son of the devil," "enemy of all righteousness," "dogs" and "swine."

The sorcerer Elymas in Acts 13 was such an enemy, as Paul states:

"You who are full of deceit and fraud, you son of the devil, you

The destruction of Jerusalem.

enemy of all righteousness, will you not cease to make
crooked the straight ways of the Lord?" (v.10 NASB)

It is recorded that the Lord blinded Elymas "for a time," as punishment and to stop his heresy, but there is no record that this temporary blindness ever led to Elymas' conversion. How could it? He was a child of Satan.

Though these enemies threaten the kingdom of God, the ultimate power belongs to Christians, as we learned when Jesus informed his seventy returning disciples:

*"Behold, I have given you authority to **tread on serpents***
***and scorpions,** and over all the power of the enemy, and*
nothing will injure you." (Luke 10:19 NASB, emphasis
added)

Jesus was not talking about literal serpents and scorpions of course. He was talking about those venomous enemies of God's kingdom. John the Baptist called them a "brood of vipers." (Matt. 3:7) Notice also the harsh power Jesus gave to His disciples: You have the authority to trample these people—to crush them.

In fact, if someone is clearly an enemy of God, it is best not to try and convert these dogs and swine at all.

"Give not that which is holy unto the dogs, neither cast your
pearls before swine, lest they trample them under their feet,
and turn again and tear you." (Matt. 7:6)

The goal is to trample *them,* not the other way around. These dogs, swine, vipers, serpents, scorpions and sons of the devil are righteous in their own eyes. Jesus did not come to call them to repentance.

"But go ye and learn what that meaneth, I will have mercy,
and not sacrifice: for I am not come to call the righteous, but
sinners to repentance." (Matt. 9:13)

The Kingdom of Heaven as a Wedding

Of particular interest is the wedding parable of Matt. 22-14. This parable speaks brilliantly of the difference among the saved, unsaved and the enemies of God.

It states that the kingdom of heaven is like a king who arranged a marriage for his son. The king sent out servants (the early Christians) to call on all those invited to the wedding. The invitation went to the Jews following the death of Christ, but the Jews were much too occupied with their farms and businesses to accept the invitation. These represent the *unsaved*. Other Jews, *the enemies of God*, not only refused to go to the wedding, but they "seized his servants, treated them spitefully, and killed them." (v. 6)

The king was disappointed with those who snubbed the wedding feast (the unsaved), but was furious at those enemies who murdered, seized and spitefully mistreated his servants.

> *"And he sent forth his armies, and destroyed those murderers, and burned up their city." (v. 7)*

This is a reference to the city of Jerusalem being destroyed by the Romans in A.D. 70.

With the city destroyed, the king told his servants to go onto the highways and "as many as you can find, invite to the wedding." These wedding invitations went to the Gentiles.

The Gentiles responded eagerly and the wedding hall was filled with guests, "both bad and good." (v.10) Yes, the wedding hall even hosted bad Christians. Why? Because they had accepted the invitation. This is a good illustration of the "once saved, always saved" argument. What is more, the "bad" were even wearing wedding garments!

Interestingly, however, the wedding hall also contained someone who was not wearing wedding garments. What was he doing there? How did he get in? The king did not know, so he asked him, "Friend, how did you come in here without wedding clothes?" (v.12)

The guest had no answer. In fact, he was speechless.

Notice the king did not criticize or question the man for being at the wedding feast with no invitation. Certainly he was invited. Everyone was invited, good and bad. It was the lack of wedding garments that aroused the suspicions of the king.

Could not the man have presented his invitation, or at least named the servant who invited him? Instead he had no answer; he could not utter a word. He had been invited but apparently never acknowledged the invitation and just showed up in his filthy clothes. He was not clothed in Christ. (Gal. 3:27) He had not put on a garment

Heartsong Church in Tennessee has opened its doors to allow Islamic services.

of righteousness. (Job 29:14)

Yet there he was mingling with all the other wedding guests, unobstructed and free to engage with everyone, until the king noticed him. The king's response was immediate: "Bind him hand and foot, take him away, and cast him into outer darkness; there shall be weeping and gnashing of teeth." (v.13)

This guest represents the enemies of God who want to enter the kingdom unlawfully, for the purpose of trying to destroy it. History is replete with such examples. But it is not as if Jesus had not warned His followers that infiltrators would try to push their way into the kingdom of God.

The parables of the Wheat and the Tares, the Mustard Seed and the Fowls, and finally the Leavened Bread all foretell of these enemy interlopers. They are similar in the respect that something foreign has been introduced and is polluting the purity of the whole. Yet each parable tells a remarkably different story.

Read those parables if you are not familiar with them: Matt. 13:24-30, 4:26-29; Mark 4:30-32 and Luke 13:21.

The Trouble with Tares

The wheat parable represents Christians working in the field of the world, as Jesus explains in Matt. 13:38. It is clear from this parable that the goal of Christians is to be in the world offering truth, salvation and the spiritual healing of Jesus to the unsaved. Yet some will enter the kingdom as bad seeds, sown by Satan himself. These tares will grow, mix in, contaminate and populate the kingdom as foreign invaders.

When the owner of the field is asked whether these tares should be removed, he tells his servants, "No, for while you are gathering up the tares, you may uproot the wheat with them." (Matt. 13.23 NASB)

To fully understand the owner's concern, tares are a species of bearded rye-grass that closely resembles wheat in its early growth. The implication is that much good wheat is closely bound to these copycat tares. So closely bound, in fact, that gathering them up could actually destroy the wheat as well. So the owner's servants (God's angels) are told to leave the tares alone until harvest.

We witness these tares mixing in the kingdom of God all the time; they are the people in our wheat field (the kingdom of God) whose single-minded purpose is to distort the truth. They can be so enmeshed with Christians that uprooting them could also uproot true believers; that is, those who are impressionable, unquestioning, gullible and fragile in faith, who have put their trust in these tares.

The mischief of these tares is to twist the truth, tell people only what they want to hear, mix in half-truths, obfuscate the scriptures, change words, change meanings, etc.

> *"For the time will come when they will not endure sound doctrine; but wanting to have their ears tickled, they will accumulate for themselves teachers in accordance to their own desires, and will turn away their ears from the truth and will turn aside to myths." (2 Tim. 4:304 NASB)*

This is reflected in some Christian denominations that now embrace abortion, homosexuality, same-sex marriages and even transsexual ministers. There are a growing number of Christians in England who now even reject the resurrection of Christ. A poll taken recently in the U.K. found that nearly one-fourth of Christians no longer believe Christ rose from the dead.

Some American churches are beginning to open their doors to Islamic services. Such was the case of the Heartsong Church in Cordova, Tenn. and the Aldersgate United Methodist Church in Alexandria, Va. Both churches allowed themselves to be turned into mosques for Friday Islamic worship. Though this practice is still rare in the United States, it is a growing trend among Christian churches in Western Europe.

Christianity is quickly becoming a mishmash of beliefs, doctrines, ceremonies, rituals— as well as exceptions and contradictions—that can make it nearly impossible for new believers to grasp what the kingdom of God actually believes and represents.

So the goal of the tares is not only to distort God's message and sow confusion, but to ultimately dominate, consume and take over God's field and make it their own.

More Parables, More Examples

Jesus foretold this effort in His parable of the Leavened Bread.
"And again he said, Whereunto shall I liken the kingdom of God? It is like leaven, which a woman took and hid in three measures of meal, till the whole was leavened." (Luke 13:20-21)

A good illustration of this bread becoming leavened was when the Roman Catholic Church was so devoured by tares in the Middle Ages that it eventually sprouted such ungodly practices as pagan worship, trial by ordeal, indulgences and the burning of Christians at the stake.

It is our Christian duty as soldiers for Christ, as warriors for Christ, to weed out these tares and resist these leavening efforts that threaten to neuter, destroy, twist and render worthless the gospel of Christ.

"Do you not know that a little leaven leavens the whole lump of dough?" the Apostle Paul asked. "Clean out the old leaven so that you may be a new lump, just as you are in fact unleavened." (1 Cor. 5:6-7 NASB)

Not only is God's kingdom being infected with tares that distort God's message and with leaven that spreads through God's kingdom, it is also being occupied by pest fowls that try to destroy Christians' faith.

This point is made in the parable of the Mustard Seed.

Jesus likens the kingdom of God to one of these seeds, which though the smallest on Earth still becomes a plant larger than all other herbs. When fully grown it puts out large branches "so that the fowls of the air may lodge under the shadow of it." (Mark 4:32)

These fowls do not represent Christians. They are as much enemies of God's kingdom as the tares in the field and the leaven mixed in with the bread dough.

In the parable, it is the branches which represent the Christians, as Jesus reveals elsewhere.

"Every branch in me that beareth not fruit he taketh away: and every branch that beareth fruit, he purgeth it, that it may bring forth more fruit." (John 15:2)

The fowls represent enemies sent by Satan, as Jesus reveals in the parable of the Sower.

In this oft-quoted parable Jesus tells of a sower who went out to sow some seed. The seed is the Word of God, sown in the hearts of man. While the owner sowed, some seed fell by the wayside "and the fowls of the air came and devoured it up." (Mark 4:4) Jesus laid blame for the hungry birds at the feet of Satan, saying, "Satan cometh immediately, and taketh away the word that was sown in their hearts." (Mark 4:15)

The fowls resting in the shadow of the mustard tree branches are no different. They are sent by Satan to snatch away the branches — the Christians who are attempting to bear fruit.

With this three-pronged attack — illustrated in the parables of the Wheat and the Tares, the Leavened Bread and the Mustard Seed — one can see how the kingdom of God is under constant assault that might only be effectively met with force.

Tares distort God's truths, message and gospel, and are notoriously hard to get rid of. Leaven attempts to take over the kingdom with its steady growth. The fowls of the air invade the hearts of Christians and try to strip out faith.

It is a classic battle of good versus evil, a battle which we are witnessing every day in our own lives.

The Eternal Conflict

The good-versus-evil conflict can be found in the storylines of countless movies, television shows, songs, Broadway plays, novels and even computer games. We see it played out on the nightly television news and in written news articles. We are on the lookout for it in our personal lives, always wary of the threat of robbery, assault, vandalism and worse. We hear about it at work, impose it on sporting events, wade into it on social media and discuss it with family members. We often make mention of the evil landlord, the thuggish football team, the scheming politician.

The eternal conflict between good and evil is part of the fabric of our lives and always has been. Virtually the entire Bible is stories of good versus evil, from the moment the serpent offers the forbidden fruit to Eve to the time of Jesus' eventual return. One would be hard-pressed to point to a single Bible verse that is not in some way wrapped around a story of good versus evil.

What is the meaning of life? The answer is all too simple and clear: It is the struggle of—and the triumph of—good over evil.

The kingdom of God suffers violence because it stands for the "good" in this endless struggle, and evil wants to win, and as we said: *violence wins.*

But what does evil really want in this battle?

Evil wants to be able to do whatever it wishes, without suffering any negative consequences. Evil desires the good things of life—joy, pleasure, intimacy, power, influence, peace of mind, material success—but seeks out these rewards through the use of mind-altering drugs (legal and illegal), alcohol, criminal activity, illicit sex, self-disfigurement and the like. Practitioners of evil have become "hardened through the deceitfulness of sin." (Heb. 3:13) and their "deceitful lusts." (Eph. 4:22). They do not like the Kingdom of God exposing these lifestyles as deceitful and as behavior ultimately leading to death, hardship, pain and misery. They want much of that Kingdom message silenced.

That is what the tares, the leaven and the fowls are doing inside the Kingdom of God; they want to control or distort that message. But the Apostle Paul warns:

> *"Know ye not that the unrighteous shall not inherit the kingdom of God? Be not deceived: neither fornicators, nor idolaters, nor adulterers, nor effeminate, nor abusers of themselves with mankind, nor thieves, nor covetous, nor drunkards, nor revilers, nor extortioners, shall inherit the kingdom of God. Such were some of you; but you were washed, but you were sanctified, but you were justified in the name of the Lord Jesus Christ and in the Spirit of our God." (1 Cor. 6:9-11)*

Elsewhere, the Apostle Paul also portrays "witchcraft, hatred, variance, emulations, wrath, strife, seditions, heresies, envyings, murders ... " as preventing people from inheriting the kingdom of God. (Gal. 5:20-21)

The operative phrase is that a person cannot *inherit* the kingdom of God unless he or she is sanctified and justified "in the name of the Lord Jesus, and by the Spirit of our God." (1 Cor. 6:11) No one inherits anything unless it is gifted by the person who died. In this case, Jesus Christ did the dying and He gifted His Kingdom only to His sons and daughters—not to tares, leaven, fowls or any other type of unbelieving infiltrator.

This is a message that evil does not want to hear. Evil wants its devilish things. Evil believes most of these wicked desires can be achieved without having to abstain, without having to suffer negative consequences, without having to be washed clean in the blood of Jesus Christ. It wants the message of the kingdom silenced, conquered or at least co-opted with its own message.

Interestingly, evil *knows* that sin has consequences. Evil knows that fornication can lead to unwanted children and disease. It knows that homosexuality can lead to AIDS. It knows that strife and anger can lead to violence and death. Evil would argue, however, that there are ways to mitigate these sufferings without having to accept the saving grace of Christ.

Evil would argue that society is well-enough equipped to handle these problems. Abortions, pills and contraceptives can prevent unwanted children, making fornication "consequence-free." Sedatives can soothe away guilt and anger. Psychiatric treatment can "cure" pedophilia. Medicine can treat AIDS. Science can deliver happiness, peace and well-being. Recovery programs can restore the drug addict. Prisons can contain the unruly and the criminal.

The Sad Impossibility of Heaven on Earth

Not all of these solutions are necessarily bad or wrong. Some are absolutely necessary if we are going to live in a society of lawlessness—prisons for instance. The point is that modern society—and those who do not want to hear or accept God's truths—believes it can solve the repercussions of evil all on its own, through human means, without any help from God.

Evil can make heaven on Earth, it thinks. Because evil does not believe in an afterlife, it actually *must*. Hence the current obsession with keeping the Earth cherished, cared-for, unviolated, managed and pristine, even at the expense of human beings. It must be preserved so that later generations can live in a harmonious and peaceful state of worldly paradise without hindrance. Earth is their God and their paradise, the only "heaven" that is attainable, though we know simply by the nature of Earthly things that this can never be. And it is not much. of a "heaven" if you can't live by an "if it feels good, do it," mentality.

So the world, that same world with which Jesus warns us not to become too friendly, must strive to find ways to handle the repercussions of sin without having to accept the message of Jesus Christ.

This world is a consummate and natural enemy of the kingdom of God. It knows there are many ways to battle its foe; that is, God's kingdom. Overwhelming strength is one way, for sure, but it is hard to do open battle with God. Infiltration is more efficient, less costly, more likely to succeed, less risky. Get in. Change the message. Keep the assets. If this does not work, resort to violence.

Regardless of the varied methods of attacking the kingdom of God, regardless of the reasons why people want in it, the kingdom has been under assault since the time of John the Baptist:

> "The Law and the Prophets were proclaimed until John; since that time the gospel of the kingdom of God has been preached, and everyone is forcing his way into it." (Luke 16:16 NASB)

CHAPTER SIX:

WHO IS AFRAID
OF FEAR?

> *Then said Jesus unto him, 'Put up again thy sword
> into his place; for all they that take the sword
> shall perish with the sword.'*
>
> (Matt. 26:52)

There is an ugly elephant in the room that no one really wants to acknowledge or talk about: Violence *wins.*

It is a brutal law of nature. We see it play out in the animal kingdom. We see it proven in war-torn lands. Violence rules the earth.

God saw it during the Antediluvian, the age before the flood:

> *"The earth also was corrupt in the sight of God, and the
> **earth was filled with violence.**" (Gen. 6:11, emphasis
> added)*

Violence is a powerful tool of the enemy. It is not tamed through rebuke, passivity, shaming or retreat. Violence is defeated only when met with an equal or greater measure of violence. This is why Jesus said, "for all they that take the sword shall perish with the sword."

Sword must be met with sword if a people are to survive. People who are willing to kill, maim, destroy or make ruin to get what they want (be it for theft, self-aggrandizement, political power, lust or religious zeal) can be stopped only if they know *they* can be killed, maimed, destroyed or brought to ruin during the attempt. There are few exceptions to this tenet of life.

Christians need to understand that if they want to stop violence directed at them, they must be willing to use violence themselves.

Those who take up the sword to get what they want cross a threshold beyond which reason, negotiation, compromise and respect are useless. They now see only force, destruction, terror and inflicting pain and death as their best and last resort for achieving their desires.

It may sound strange, but it is doubtful Christ was making a statement of condemnation when he told Peter that those "who take the sword shall perish with the sword." He was simply stating the truth and neither approving nor disapproving of it.

That is because the truth behind the statement swings both ways. Violence must be met with violence. Hitler was willing to use violence in his zeal to establish the Third Reich. The Allies were willing to use violence to stop him. Both sides knew that once swords were drawn, neither side was going to stop until one side was violently defeated.

The Power of Fear

We have already examined several places in the New Testament where authorities feared the response of disciples and multitudes if they tried using violence against Jesus, John the Baptist or the Apostles. The rulers knew that if they took up the sword against these religious figures, they too would be met with the "sword" (more likely stones and clubs) by their defenders.

The authorities *feared* those disciples and multitudes.

Regrettably, people no longer fear Christians.

Instilling fear in an opponent is a tremendous weapon of persuasion, whether it seems like a nice idea or not. Fear can be witnessed persuading others throughout the Bible, from Genesis to Revelation.

Of course it does not always work. God tried to instill fear in Adam when He told him not to eat from the tree of the knowledge of good and evil. " ... in the day that thou eatest thereof thou shalt surely die." (Gen. 2:17) Adam should have listened.

But Jesus spoke of the fearful consequences in store for those who refuse to repent, saying an "unquenchable fire" awaits them. The Apostle Paul told people to be fearful of "God's wrath" if they have an "unrepentant heart."

Revelation is full of fearful consequences for sinners, whom God calls "the dogs, those who practice magic arts, the sexually immoral, the murderers, the idolaters and everyone who loves and practices falsehood." (Rev. 22:14 NIV)

The Bible encourages us all to "fear the Lord." (Ps. 34:9)

Conservative Congressman Steve Scalise was critically injured by a shooter who disagreed with his views.

Make no mistake; God uses fear as one of His many tools of persuasion.

We are all vulnerable to fear. It is how God made us. It can be a good or bad thing, depending on the situation. Sometimes it is best to give in to fear; sometimes one must hold fast even when terrified. Everyone should have a healthy fear of tornadoes, swarming wasps, going through a railroad crossing while the lights are flashing. There is nothing wrong with that. But no one should ever fear doing God's will, no matter how dangerous a situation looks. We should never allow fear to stop us from doing what we know to be God's work.

The enemies of God are well aware that fear is a powerful emotional instrument that can paralyze their foes. They will attempt to use fear as a battering ram against those who try to uphold the truths of God.

This is why the Bible is replete with phrases telling God's people not to fear man. Among them are:

"Be strong, do not fear … " (Isaiah 35:4) " … do not be afraid." (John 14:27) "Do not fear their threats … " (1 Peter 3:14) "I will fear no evil … " (Ps. 23:4) "he delivered me from all my fears." (Ps. 34:4)

It was for good reason that the Bible offers this encouragement. Without the ability to create fear among God's people, the enemy has very little power.

Unfortunately the world—including God's people—is caving in to fear. God's enemies have orchestrated multiple platforms of fear that can seem, in combination, overwhelming and crushing.

Political Correctness as a Tool of Fear

The issue of political correctness is an excellent example.

Political correctness is the attempt to shame people for using certain words or phrases on the basis that the language is offensive, derogatory, discriminatory, racist or the like.

Its basic strategy is to instill fear in the "offending" person—to make him fear being ostracized, discredited or embarrassed unless he changes the way he expresses himself to others. Unless he changes the very *way he thinks.*

If this fear tactic is not persuasive enough, then the next step could be to get that person fired from his job or get him fined, sent to jail, subjected to a lawsuit, even physically assaulted or worse. All of these levers have been used to silence opposing conservative voices.

In New York City, a person can now be fined up to $250,000 for repeatedly uttering the wrong pronoun when referring to a transgender person.

In California, health care workers who repeatedly direct the wrong pronoun toward a transgender person can face both a $1,000 fine and "Imprisonment in the county jail for a period not to exceed one year," or both.

In Georgia, a fire chief, Kelvin Cochran, was fired after he wrote a book expressing his religious view that homosexuality is "vile" and "vulgar."

In Queens, NY, pro-life protesters were sued by an attorney general who claimed their message outside an abortion clinic was meant to "harass and menace" clinic customers.

Outside Washington, D.C., James Hodgkinson opened fire on a congressional GOP baseball practice, critically injuring congressman Steve Scalise, who was an outspoken pro-life, pro-family majority whip of the U.S. House of Representatives.

These are just a few examples of how God's enemies attempt to instill fear in their opponents. Their goal is to silence and gag their critics. They know that no one wants to be sued, jailed, fined, fired, beaten, arrested or even shot at for standing up for his or her opinions.

The temptation to keep one's mouth shut in the face of these harsh retributions can be overwhelming, unless one approaches these enemies as King David did:

> *"The LORD is on my side; I will not fear: what can man do unto me?" (Ps. 118:6)*

The Israelites Fall Victim to Fear

An important lesson in becoming a Christian warrior is that you cannot succumb to fear.

The Bible offers numerous stories of His chosen being led into fearful situations. Those who stood strong despite their fear were rewarded. Those who buckled were often punished, sometimes severely.

The Israelites feared Pharaoh's army during their Exodus from Egypt, but were promised a reward if they completed the journey. They would inherit a land flowing with milk and honey, Moses told them. When they arrived at the Wilderness of Paran, Moses sent out twelve spies to investigate this Promised Land, also known as Canaan:

> *"See what the land is like, and whether the people who live in it are strong or weak, whether they are few or many. How is the land in which they live, is it good or bad? And how are the cities in which they live, are they like open camps or with fortifications?" (Num. 13:18-19 NASB)*

Moses knew it would be a dangerous and fearful mission, so he told them, "Be of good courage."

Students of the Bible are familiar with what happened next, as detailed in Numbers chapters 13 and 14. After journeying for forty days in the land of Canaan, the twelve spies returned with their findings. They all agreed that the land "flows with milk and honey," but ten of them also said it was a land that "devours its inhabitants."

Canaan is made up of "men of great stature," they reported. The people were "strong" and "fortified." Particularly alarming was the sight of "the descendants of Anak," who were considered giants. These titans made the spies look like grasshoppers in their own eyes. Their conclusion: "We are not able to go up against the people, for they are stronger than we."

Their fear spread throughout the camp. "If only we had died in the land of Egypt!" people cried. "Or if only we had died in the wilderness." (They would soon get their wish.)

Only two of the returning spies gave a favorable report. Joshua and Caleb told the Israelites, " … the Lord is with us. Do not fear them." But the damage was already done. Israel had succumbed to fear.

Most Christians of today might expect God to be understanding, since He is a patient and forgiving God. Israel was, after all, being asked to fight well-trained giants in a fortified land that devours its *own* people, whereas the Israelites were a ragtag army with just one previous battle under its belt, a brief skirmish with the Amalekites. Even that battle was a defensive action. Israel had to fight or die.

But to *attack?* Israel was more accustomed to fleeing from armies than engaging them.

At the human level, Israel's fear of the Canaanites made sense. The Israelites were not skilled soldiers. They were shepherds whose only other notable skills were making bricks and mixing mortar. They were not trained, experienced warriors. They were all too familiar with the might of the Egyptian army and they knew what it was like to confront an overpowering enemy. Fleeing had to seem the better part of valor. Which is exactly what they did when they left Egypt.

Now God wanted them to fight against giants? Did God really want them to "fall by the sword, that our wives and children should become victims? Would it not be better for us to return to Egypt?" they asked.

God was not just a little angry over their fear of going up against the Canaanites. He was so outraged He wanted to kill them.

"I will strike them with pestilence and disinherit them," God said, and were it not for the intercession of Moses, He mostly likely would have killed them all.

King David would later describe God as being "furious." (Ps. 78:21) And God had good reason to be.

How could the Israelites succumb to fear after all the miracles He had previously shown them? Did all the miracles that occurred in Egypt mean nothing—the plagues, a river that was turned into blood,

The black flag of Al Qaeda. "When a Muslim says, 'I'm going to plant the black flag on the White House,' why is everyone so surprised?"

the death of all the first born of Egypt? These meant nothing?

What about the parting of the Red Sea or the cloud and fire that guided them day and night through the desert? Did they forget about the rock that was split open so that water gushed out and they could drink? Even the sky told of His miraculous powers. Food fell from heaven six days a week.

Did they not remember their victory over the Amalekites? How about the Egyptian army that was swallowed up by the Red Sea? Was all this forgotten by the Israelites?

Lack of faith was on full display at the Wilderness of Paran, and it was all because of one thing: *fear*.

Though God relented on His impulse to destroy the entire congregation of Israelites, He did send a plague that killed the spies giving the bad report. He punished everyone twenty years old and above by denying them the privilege of ever entering the Promised Land. These souls would remain stuck in in the desert for the next forty years, until they died, just as they wished for. Such were the consequences of giving in to fear. Joshua and Caleb, however, who gave the more optimistic and courageous report, were promised entry into the Promised Land.

The symbolism of this story should be clear to Christians. Fear kept the Israelites out of the Promised Land. Do we want God to keep us out of our Promised Land, a land flowing with milk and honey; that is, God's rest?

> *"Therefore I swore in My anger, 'Truly they shall not enter into My rest.' " (Ps. 95:11 NASB)*

The enemy wants us to live in fear: fear of lawsuits, jail, firings, fines, mistreatment and violence. They want to neuter us and keep our faith chained inside our homes. These hypocrites want to infiltrate our kingdom with their lies, which they do. And we had better never try to infiltrate their secular institutions or chambers with our truths.

Islam's Use of Fear

It is not just the secularist enemy who wants to strike fear into Christians, is it? Radical Islam also knows how to use fear as a weapon, though it wants to strike fear into everyone (Christian and non-Christian alike) who does not follow the teachings of Allah and the fake prophet Muhammad.

Their goal is world domination.

In our documentary film *Europe's Last Stand: America's Final Warning,* we traveled to Western Europe to expose the rise of Islam in those nations and the Islamic effort to conquer European populations and governments. We visited a dozen countries and interviewed everyone from people on the street to politicians, religious leaders and Muslim radicals.

One of the most striking interviews we were able to obtain was with Abu Imran, the spokesman for Sharia4Belgium, a designated terrorist organization. Abu now sits in a Belgian jail for inciting hatred against non-Muslims, but we had a chance to interview him shortly before his arrest. He told us:

> *"We have the black flag of Islam. People call it the flag of Al Qaeda. Al Qaeda are Muslims. You have the American flag*

and you people went to the moon and planted the American flag. So when a Muslim says, 'I'm going to plant the black flag on the White House,' why is everyone so surprised?

"What's more crazy? Planting a black flag on the White House or planting an American flag on the moon? I'm just asking the question.

"So with the Islamic flag, we believe Islam will dominate the world. And of course, we have our flags? America is falling apart. It's going down. So if the American people want to save themselves, I think Sharia (Islamic law) is a good solution."

Abu claimed that it is worthless for Islam to try to work within democracy to change the system. "You can't break a system with a system," he said. "You throw away the system and install a new system. That's Sharia. And that's what we believe."

He is not alone in the Muslim world, as we all know by watching the news. He is backed by thousands if not millions of Muslims who support subduing the world through violence—using commercial planes, trucks, swords, guns, bombs, knives and even pressure cookers to kill, maim and terrorize non-Muslims.

The chief desire of these radical Islamists is to put fear into their enemies, which is what the Quran teaches:

> *"I will cast terror into the hearts of those who disbelieve. Therefore strike off their heads and strike off every fingertip of them." (Quran 8:12)*

Fear and Today's Christians

In today's world, Christians do not have to go looking for fearful situations. Fearful situations now come directly to them if they dare to stand for God's truths.

In our work at the Christian Action Network, we have been placed in many fearful, violent and potentially deadly situations.

We once set out to deliver petitions to the United Nations in New York City. The petitions came from thousands of Americans who opposed the United States' involvement with this international organization. Prior to delivering the petitions we arranged a time, date and place for a particular U.N. official to accept delivery. Everything was arranged. It should have been smooth sailing.

After arriving at the U.N.'s New York headquarters in Manhattan, however, the official changed his mind and refused to meet with us. We were obviously upset, both at his unprofessional behavior and at his backing away from his promise. We had spent thousands of dollars to gather these signed petitions, as well as paid a hefty sum to travel to New York with half a dozen staff members.

Was all this for nothing?

I stood at the top of the U.N. steps, surrounded by armed security guards, demanding the official keep his promise and accept our bags of petitions.

The response of the guards was swift and violent. They lifted me into the air and threw me down the stone steps headfirst. When the police arrived they arrested me and put me in jail, even though I was injured. I was charged with disorderly conduct. It was a false and unfounded charge, but I spent several hours behind bars before being released. Several weeks later, when I arrived at court to face those phony charges, prosecutors dropped the case without explanation.

An Unforgettable Day of Fear

Eventually, after we embarrassed the U.N. with an aggressive media campaign, U.N. officials relented and once again agreed to accept our citizen petitions. The meeting was set for a specific date: September 11, 2001. Our staff received a phone call early that morning, at about 8 a.m., from the U.N. Public Affairs Office. Once again our meeting was being canceled. At least this time, however, it was with an acceptable excuse: A plane had just crashed into the North Tower of the World Trade Center.

Sheikh Mubarak Ali Gilani.

New York City seemed to be under attack, especially when a second aircraft struck the South Tower a short while later. The government issued warnings that more commandeered planes with suicidal pilots could be on the way. Military fighter jets roared over our heads. It was eerie.

For the next several days our entire staff was trapped on the island of Manhattan after bridges, tunnels, train stations and all passenger air travel were shut down.

The co-author of this book, Jerry Skirvin, was there with me. Together we understood this Islamic attack was against American values, prosperity and yes, even Christianity. We realized that Christians would want to know more about this enemy. Who were they? What did they believe? What do they want? Where are they? Why do they want to kill us and destroy our cultural icons?

It escaped neither Jerry nor me that delving into the area of radical Islam could be dangerous.

A little more than a year after the World Trade Center crumbled into dust, America witnessed the dreadful beheading of *Wall Street Journal* reporter Daniel Pearl, who was kidnapped while investigating a radical Islamist living in Pakistan, Sheikh Mubarak Ali Gilani.

I remember that while watching the video of Pearl's decapitation I said to myself, "At least God hasn't asked me to go to Pakistan and deal with those lunatics."

Little did I know.

A God-given Task

As our organization set out to expose Islam and its assorted radical networks in America, we produced and distributed thousands of informational pamphlets and held special grassroots events to expose the jihadi goal of domination. I had long ago put the gruesome image of Pearl's beheading out of my thoughts. I was more concerned about radical Islam in the United States, not Islamic butchery happening in foreign countries 7,000 miles away.

But in 2006, while we were hosting a conference on Islam in Washington, D.C., a gentleman by the name of Paul Williams approached me, introducing himself as a former consultant to the FBI.

"You may want to be careful about holding these events," he said. "You have an Islamic terrorist camp just thirty miles from your office."

He was right. In Red House, Va. (about an hour's drive from the CAN office) there was a fully functional camp operating under the name of Muslims of America (MOA).

What I would learn was that MOA had nearly two dozen Islamic camps scattered around the country—from Florida to New York, from South Carolina to California, from Michigan to Texas.

In an MOA recruitment video that we were able to obtain through a confidential source, we discovered that the group was planning to establish guerilla warfare training camps throughout America, and that the group was reaching out to American Muslims to join.

"You are most welcome to join one of the most advanced training courses in Islamic military warfare," said MOA's leader and founder in the film.

That leader was none other than Sheikh Mubarak Ali Gilani, the very person Daniel Pearl was attempting to interview in Pakistan when he was kidnapped and later beheaded. Now I learned that one of his camps was just thirty miles from our office doors.

So much for God not asking me to deal with "those lunatics."

The decision at Christian Action Network was to go about exposing MOA and their American-based terrorist camps in a feature-length documentary film. I spoke to a military intelligence officer who was familiar with our organization about our plans and he told me: "If you don't leave them alone, they're going to cut your head off."

Only someone who was completely insane would have had no fear entering into this film project, and it goes without saying that the gruesome image of Daniel Pearl's beheading, long since buried, found its way back into the front of our minds. We were certain, though, that God wanted CAN to expose MOA and its reclusive, sinister and flourishing guerilla training compounds.

For the next several years we put our full resources into uncovering America's largest network of Islamic terrorist camps. In 2009 we released a film about them, *Homegrown Jihad.* In 2012 I released a book about them called *Twilight in America,* co-authored with Patti A. Pierucci.

Both the book and film received domestic and international coverage. The Islamic group was no longer able to operate in secret, quietly building camps under the radar in the United States. We exposed such domestic terrorist attacks conducted by MOA as kidnapping, murder, assassinations, fire-bombings, their involvement in the first World Trade Center bombing in 1993 and their plot to blow up bridges in New York City.

As we increasingly exposed their United States operations to scrutiny from law enforcement, media and the public, MOA was forced to change its strategy. Rather than conducting terrorism inside America, they adopted a more international focus. They formed criminal gangs in the United States to raise money through illegal gun sales and drug operations. Some members used unemployment and welfare scams to raise cash. The accumulated money was sent back to Sheikh Gilani in Pakistan to fund global terrorism.

MOA members were angry over the heat we brought down upon them. In 2014 they filed a $35 million lawsuit against us, claiming we libeled and defamed them. The lawsuit employed such scare tactics as demanding to know the home addresses of our employees and board members, the phones and computers we were using and the locations of our bank accounts. They wanted to know the names and addresses of our confidential informants, including the names and addresses of family members.

Going Ahead Despite the Fear

They were using fear as a tactic to halt my exposure of their North American operations. Their message was clear: Either stop the scrutiny of our organization or face an expensive lawsuit; pay up to $35 million in damages; and turn over the names and addresses of those you love to a terrorist group.

I knew it was God who directed my heart to shed light on the history and activities of MOA. I was called and directed by God for this purpose, much like Moses directed his spies to cross over into Canaan and make a report. Was MOA strong or weak? Few or many? Were they in places like camps or strongholds?

My report probably sounded very similar to that of the spies who returned from Canaan. MOA was strong. They were well-trained. They were fortified. They too had a history of killing their opponents and devouring their own. I became an annoying mosquito in the eyes of MOA leaders, a tiny bug that they felt they could squash, intimidate and bring into submission through a lawsuit.

But our organization did not buckle or break. We fought back and eventually won the lawsuit when a federal judge in New York dismissed MOA's legal claim in 2015, but not before the whole action cost our organization $180,000 in legal fees.

Of course this did not stop MOA from coming after me. Their options for retribution became fewer but no less threatening.

Not long after MOA's lawsuit was thrown out of court, our office received a call from a member of MOA who wanted to become a confidential informant. I cannot give details for fear of putting this person at risk of exposure and retribution; neither can I confirm whether the individual is male or female. For the purposes of this book, I will refer to this informant only as "X."

X wanted to meet me to disclose the criminal activities of Muslims of America. I agreed to the meeting, knowing very little about X other than a description of this person's physical appearance. I would meet with X at a hotel for two days and have the most intimate details of MOA described to me—their gun running, drug dealing, killings, internal discipline, military training, officers, ranks and more.

The first thing X wanted me to know, however, was that MOA intended to kill me.

"You have a warrant on your head," X said. "They want to kill you. First chance they get is to kill you. They're not going to maim you. They're not going to just whip up on you. They're going to kill you."

When I asked how they planned to accomplish my demise, X said,

"They are going to shoot the s*** out of you wherever they see you. That's because you brought the heat onto them. So just be on your P's and Q's, because they are very determined about doing it. Really watch yourself. I'm not going to say anything is going to happen next month. I'm not going to say it's going to happen to you next year."

As X explained it, MOA first wants to get things turned around, get the government off their backs, before coming after me.

"Then they are going to come for you. They want to kill you. They want to get the feds to fall back off of them, get them off the terrorist list. Then after they do all that, they are going to come for you."

Do I fear that they will attempt to kill me? Yes, I do. They once killed a Muslim cleric in Tucson, Ariz. over a minor religious dispute involving the Quran. The murderers hid in the kitchen of Rashad Khalifa's mosque one morning and then stabbed him seventeen times after he entered.

I have seen training manuals given to MOA members with instructions on how to stake out houses, disable security alarms, cut power lines and break into homes to kill opponents.

In their official recruitment video, called *Soldiers of Allah*, MOA tells its members, "Act like you're a friend and then kill them."

That is exactly what happened to Dr. Mozaffar Ahmad of Canton, Mich. MOA members went to dinner with him and showered him with pleasantries. After the meal was over MOA members followed Dr. Ahmad to his home, where they shot him and set his house on fire. (MOA had a religious disagreement with Dr. Ahmad as well.)

Because they are willing to harm anyone, including their own, it is only natural to feel fear toward MOA. Still, using many figures appearing in the Bible as my inspiration, I refuse to let fear divert me from doing God's will.

The parents of Moses hid him as a baby for three months, "because they saw he was a beautiful child; and they were **not afraid** of the king's command." (Hebrews 11:23 NASB, emphasis added)

Moses would eventually leave Egypt, **"not fearing the wrath of the king"** (Hebrews 11:27 NASB, emphasis added).

There is little doubt that Caleb and Joseph had justifiable fear upon entering a land prowled by giants who devoured their own. Still, they trusted in God and were not afraid.

It is not possible to defend God's truths and be free of fear, especially when lawsuits, possible imprisonment, loss of employment, public humiliation, hefty fines and even violence may be the result.

In truth, the enemies of God should fear us and not the other way around. It bears repeating that Jewish leaders "feared the people" when they plotted against both John the Baptist and Jesus Christ. If the enemy knows you are afraid, they will step up their terror against you.

MOA wants to scare me. Apparently they would like to kill me. But they also fear me. They know if they murder me all hell will break loose on their criminal organizations and their illegal revenue stream for global jihadi terrorism will dry up.

"If something were to happen to you right now," X told me, "it would bring back the heat on MOA. But if the government starts to go lax on them, watch yourself."

Do Not Be Afraid of Goliath

We do not have to delve too deep into scripture to find stories of heroism in the face of fear. Perhaps the best-known and most often recounted is David's battle against Goliath. As all of Israel succumbed to fear, a ruddy-faced kid carrying nothing but a sling, with no previous battle experience, took on a 6'9" giant carrying a bronze sword and wearing a bronze helmet and a coat of mail weighing seventy-eight pounds. If that was not enough to smite the little fellow approaching him with a handful of rocks, Goliath carried a javelin between his shoulders that he could have hurled at David.

Most will remember this story as a display of courage and faith, not to mention incredible skill. It should also be remembered for something else:

It showed what the courage of one person can do to defeat God's enemies.

CHAPTER SEVEN:

OUR REAL ROLE HERE ON EARTH

> *Be fruitful and multiply; fill the earth and subdue it.*
> *(Gen. 1:29)*

The history of mankind is unfolding just how God planned it would. It Is a story of man on a crusade to subdue the Earth and make it a bondservant of his collective will. Both the godly and the godless have taken up this challenge. Wars have been fought, and continue to be fought, to accomplish this great mission of conquest. In its simplest terms, subduing the Earth is a centuries-long effort to mold our planet according to the desires of man—whether for good or evil, whether for God or Satan. These are the only two options, and from them all else follows.

This mission is not just a battle for land, but also for ideas, commerce, discovery, construction, formation, growth, consumption and the many other tangible and intangible commodities that our wonderful Earth has to offer.

As Christians we know that the Earth, including all that it contains and all those who dwell in it, belongs to the Lord. (Ps. 24:1) But Satan, who is the god of this world (2 Cor. 4:4), also battles for the right to control the future of Earth.

The battle lines are easily discernible.

Our mission as Christians is to subdue the Earth and bring it into alignment with God's will. Along the way (as history has shown) there will be fierce enemies who will attempt to stop us and, if possible, swallow us up in fear and death. This should not be a mystery to us.

> *"If the world hates you, you know that it has hated Me before*
> *it hated you." (John 15:18 NASB)*

That hatred brings about persecution:

"Indeed, all who desire to live godly in Christ Jesus will be persecuted." (2 Tim. 3:12 NASB)

Notice that the word is "all," not "some." For none who attempt to subdue the Earth for Christ and His Father will be exempt from persecution. The point of that persecution will be for Satan to fill us with dread, panic and horror at attempting to do so. Since there is no escaping persecution, it takes courage to subdue the Earth.

The author of Hebrews knew this and heaped praises on biblical figures who refused to cower in fear when confronted with worldly enemies. He mentions Rahab, Gideon, Barak, Samson, Jephthah, David and Samuel by name. (Hebrews 11:31-32) He talks about others who were tortured, scourged, mocked, chained, imprisoned, stoned, sawn in two and slain with the sword.

He gave them high praise because they "subdued kingdoms, worked righteousness, obtained promises, stopped the mouths of lions, quenched the violence of fire, escaped the edge of the sword." They may have begun in "weakness," Hebrews' author writes, but through faith they were "made strong, became valiant in battle" and "turned to flight the armies of aliens." (Hebrews 11:33-34)

We see, therefore, our goal as Christians who are also citizens of Earth. We are to subdue kingdoms, work righteousness, obtain promises, stop the mouths of lions, quench violence and escape the edge of the sword. We are to be valiant in battle and make armies turn to flight. The enemies are "aliens" who must be conquered; they have no right to rule the Earth. It belongs to God.

The author of Hebrews would not have sung high praises of these Old Testament figures if their deeds had been meant for a different time period. The author gives us examples of courageous individuals to follow. We cannot cherry-pick these verses and say some accomplishments were meant for a different time and age and some for now.

If we throw out the author's praise of *subduing kingdoms*, then we must also throw out his praise of *working righteousness*. If we discard his praise for being *valiant in battle*, then we must also discard his praise for *obtaining promises*. Who's to dispute that it is our Christian mission is to "stop the mouths of lions" and "quench the violence of fire"?

On the whole, Hebrews' author sums up nicely our duties before God and our responsibility as human beings. God created us to rule the earth, not in the sense of ruling from a Christian theocracy, but certainly with the aim of ruling with Christian principles, truths, values and ethics. Which is exactly how the United States was founded.

Rep. Steve Scalise, mentioned in the last chapter as having been shot and nearly killed while attending a GOP baseball practice, has said this while serving as the majority whip of the U.S. House of Representatives:

> *"This was a nation founded with a deep belief in God. Our Founding Fathers talked about it when they were preparing to draft the Constitution …*

> *"Faith is part of who you are. It is part of who I am, it is part of what establishes the values that I bring to this job and I would hope that everybody brings a set of values rooted in faith when they're making consequential decisions that don't just affect our country **but affect the entire world.**" (National Prayer Breakfast, February 8, 2018, emphasis added)*

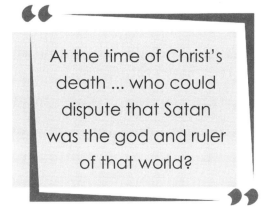

> At the time of Christ's death ... who could dispute that Satan was the god and ruler of that world?

Subduing the Earth for God and Christianity, imparting eternal truths to the entire world, ruling with a set of values that are rooted in faith, making disciples of all nations, even risking death (as Scalise did)—this is our great commission.

The 'God of this World'

Often Christians treat the words "Earth" and "world" as having similar meanings. Because scripture says Satan is the "god of this world," it may lead us to believe that Satan is somehow "god of the Earth" as well. He is not. There are several Bible passages that can lead us into this misunderstanding of Satan's role on Earth.

The first is in 2 Cor. 4:4, where Paul says in reference to Satan:

> *"In whom the **god of this world** hath blinded the minds of them which believe not, lest the light of the glorious gospel of Christ, who is the image of God, should shine unto them." (emphasis added)*

The second is found in the story of Jesus after He was tempted for 40 days and nights in the wilderness:

> *"And the devil, taking him up into an high mountain, shewed unto him all the **kingdoms of the world** in a moment of time. And the devil said unto him, 'All this power will I give thee, and the glory of them: **for that is delivered unto me**; and to whomsoever I will I give it.' " (Luke 4:5-6, emphasis added)*

The third comes after the Jews heard a voice from heaven after Jesus prayed to God to "glorify your name." (John 21:28)

> *"Now judgment is upon this world; now the **ruler of this world** will be cast out." (John 12:31, NASB, emphasis added)*

From these verses we learn that Satan is not only the "god" and "ruler" of the world, but claims he can give that power, and its kingdoms, to whomever he wishes. Before reviewing these scriptures giving Satan such remarkable ownership of the world and its kingdoms, it would be wise to examine exactly what else scripture has to say about the Prince of Darkness.

Since the Bible was never meant to be a story about Satan, it's not surprising there is so little information about him. We know that he roams the Earth, walking back and forth on it. He has been described as a roaring lion with an insatiable appetite for devouring people. He can cast humans into prison and make them suffer illness and death. He is a murderer who can both oppress and possess people. Because he is a thief, he can steal the word of God out of the hearts of men.

The Angel of Darkness can actually present himself as an angel of light. He never tires of tempting God's people into sin and then accusing them before their Maker. He has the power to weaken nations and cause destruction. Being the father of lies and deception, he can cause man to lie and deceive. Finally, because Satan knows his time is short, he uses his great wrath to make the earth tremble and its kingdoms shake.

These are the works of Satan, which Jesus Christ came to destroy.

"The Son of God appeared for this purpose, to destroy the works of the devil." (1 John 3:8 NASB)

Since we are to be "imitators" of Christ (1 Cor. 11:1), follow His "example" (1 Peter 2:21) and "walk in the same manner" as Christ (1 John 2:6), this should be our purpose as well — to destroy the works of the devil. This might seem futile, however, if we believe Satan will be the "god" and "ruler" of this world until Christ's return, which he most certainly will be, though he will never be god of this Earth.

How Can Satan's Works be Destroyed?

This is where it becomes important to understand what it means when Scripture talks about Satan being the "god of this world." Notice, nowhere in Scripture is Satan referred to as "god of this Earth." The Earth belongs to God along with all that dwell within it. God unquestionably rules over the Earth. But it is Satan who unquestionably rules over the "world."

When the Bible speaks of the "world" in reference to Satan's power and ownership, it is referring to the *world of unbelievers*: all those who do not accept Jesus Christ as their Lord and Savior. Satan is their "god" and rules over them, as well as over the kingdoms they control.

So when Scripture says that Satan is the "god of this world" or the "ruler of this world," it should be interpreted no differently than if one were to say, "Allah is the god of all Muslims and the ruler over their kingdoms."

As the Apostle John made clear, "the whole world lies under the sway of the wicked one." (1 John 5:19) We know that Christians do not live under the sway of Satan, so John's reference to the "whole world" refers to non-Christians only. Therefore, the more we "destroy the works of the devil," the smaller Satan's "world" becomes on Earth.

At the time of Christ's death, and at the start of the Great Commission, this "world" basically consumed the entire Earth. During the Apostolic Age, there were but a small number of Christians against a whole world of Gentiles. Who could dispute that Satan was the god and ruler of that world? Through the centuries, however, that "world" would shrink as the message of the Gospel spread and Christians began subduing the earth.

The Old Testament duties of "subduing the earth" did not change for Christians when Christ died on the cross. In fact, the death and resurrection of Christ gave *power* to Christians to use in subduing the earth.

The duties of man are found in the very first chapter of the Bible, which makes sense. An employer does not wait until a worker has been on the job for years before explaining to that worker what his duties are, and neither does God. He made man and then immediately explained man's duties while engaging the Earth.

First we learn that we are made in the likeness and image of God, which means that (just like God) we have the ability to think and strategize; plan and be creative; direct and give order to chaos; be inventive and calculating; learn and discover. In other words, we have the skills to *subdue*.

The 'Age of Dechristianization," also known as the 'Cult of Reason.'

93

It is no coincidence that right after God made man in His image, He gave man dominion over the fish, birds, cattle and every creeping and living thing that moves on the Earth.

Then we come to this very important piece of Scripture. It is the very first commandment given by God to man:

"Be fruitful and multiply, and fill the earth, and subdue it."
(Gen. 1:28 NASB)

The Hebrew word for subdue is *kabash*, which means to bring into subjection, force into bondage and tread under our foot. From the day man was created, this was our purpose: to subdue the Earth.

A Duty to Subdue

It is both ironic and sad that the enemies of God appear to have accepted and risen to this challenge more seriously than present-day Christians. Christians do not rule the media, the entertainment industry, the government, the arts, the courts or the education system as a whole, and each of these power centers has become corrupted and twisted to the purpose of subduing the earth *and* Christians. This is not to say there are not many fine Christians to be found in each of these fields, but it is clear that Christians do not dominate any of them even partially.

In the past, many have considered America to be a Promised Land, something worth subduing. Nathan Hale, who would later be hanged for acting as a spy under General George Washington, once wrote in a letter to a friend, "I consider our country a land, flowing as it were, with milk and honey."

John Quincy Adams, the sixth president of the United States, understood as a Christian that America was worth subduing:

*"The highest, the transcendent glory of the American Revolution was this—it connected, in one indissoluble bond, the principles of civil government **with the precepts of Christianity**." (John Quincy Adams, April 27, 1837, emphasis added)*

We may look at the current state of our nation and consider America too far gone, too steeped in debauchery, too godless. Some believe America has become a country more deserving of God's wrath than His salvation. Evangelist Anne Graham Lotz, the granddaughter of Billy Graham, has even asked, "Is God's judgment coming on America?"

All of this, unfortunately, is typical of modern-day Christian thinking. Rather than going out and conquering and reclaiming our Promised Land, we will instead wait for God's wrath to take care of this nasty bit of business for us, as if our duty as Christians to "subdue kingdoms" and "stop the mouths of lions" ended with the death of Christ.

We should thank God that our Founding Fathers were not the type of Christians who waited on the wrath of God to free America from British tyranny.

Christians were created for a spiritual purpose and an earthly purpose. We are to offer our spirit and soul to a living God who demands righteousness from us, and we are to offer our human bodies for subduing the earth *into* righteousness. For if we are to "live for righteousness" (1 Peter 2:24), it helps if we live in a righteous nation.

"Righteousness exalteth a nation: but sin is a reproach to any people." (Prov. 14:34)

A righteous nation does not happen by accident and it certainly does not happen as a result of God's wrath. What nation ever turned to righteousness following an earthquake, hurricane or a tsunami? The Bible shows us that a culture suffering the wrath of God is far from being transformed into a righteous nation. It is far more likely being transformed into extinction.

The biblical flood reformed no one. It did wipe out every person on Earth save eight people, Noah and his family. The fire and brimstone that rained down on Sodom and Gomorrah destroyed those cities; it didn't reform anyone. The people were turned into ash. The ten plagues sent to Egypt were never meant to convert the Egyptians into a righteous nation. They were meant to force Egypt to free the Israelites, and Egyptians paid dearly for their stubborn refusal.

If a nation is to be righteous, it will come as a result of Christians who dare to subdue it. If the godless rule over the nation, the result will be sin, which will bring reproach upon all the people.

France's Nightmare of Ungodly Rule

Such was the case in France during the "Age of Dechristianiza-tion," which occurred during the French Revolution. During this nearly 12-year period, the religious citizens of France experienced the harsh reality of living under a government controlled by the godless.

Priests were required to swear an oath of loyalty to the newly formed revolutionary government, which proudly boasted of its atheism. If the oath were not sworn, the priest faced exile, imprisonment or death. Churches were nationalized and their land was seized. Many churches were either auctioned off to the public or converted into so-called "Temples of Reason."

The new state religion became known as the Cult of Reason. This religion rejected any belief in a Supreme Being or other gods. Human reasoning itself became the god to worship.

Christian statues, plates and other religious symbols and tools were destroyed, including crosses and bells. Christian processions in the streets were banned. Wearing the Cross became a crime. Religious dress was forbidden. Street names with Christian connotations were changed. Religious holidays were banned.

Even the Gregorian calendar was changed from a seven-day-week calendar to a 10-day-week calendar, so great was the hatred for anything Christian. The word "Sunday" was formally banned in October 1793. (The Gregorian calendar was later restored when workers protested a nine-day workweek and when it became impossible to do business with other nations while using a different calendar.)

To commemorate its new Cult of Reason, the government held a festival that took place in November 1793 at the cathedral of Notre Dame in Paris. Historians describe that celebration as "lurid," "licentious" and full of scandalous "depravities."

One of the government officials, Joseph Foché, ordered that signs on all cemetery gates be changed to carry the inscription, "Death is an eternal sleep," because there is no God.

Just a year prior to the Age of Dechristianization, in 1792, the church was already viewed as a counter-revolutionary force. During a 48-hour period in September of that year, three bishops were killed

Abram and Lot.

and more than 200 priests were drowned by mobs. The slayings became known as the September Massacres. Other priests were forced onto ships as prisoners. Of the 827 priests imprisoned only 285 survived; most died from starvation, thirst or the filthy conditions.

Public worship would not return to France until Feb. 21, 1795, when Napoleon met with Pope Pius VII and formally ended the dechristianization period. Christian crosses were still forbidden, however, and it would take another century to do away with most other anti-church laws.

Known as the "Reign of Terror," the dechristianization period would claim between 20,000 to 40,000 lives, with workers and peasants making up 70 percent of the deaths.

Like modern-day enemies of God, these atheists believed they had discovered a "virtue" that all should accept—a society without God where human reason prevailed. They clearly were willing to kill, banish or imprison those who disagreed.

One of the most influential leaders of the French Revolution was Maximilien Robespierre, who believed that the "virtue" of human reason was so important it needed to be violently enforced, even through terror if necessary. "Virtue," Robespierre said, "without which terror is baneful; terror, without which virtue is powerless. Terror is nothing more than speedy, severe and inflexible justice; it is thus an emanation of virtue."

So there you have it, according to Robespierre. You cannot have virtue without terror to enforce it. Terror is speedy, severe, inflexible. We should not be surprised, therefore, that modern-day secularists and atheists also believe that terror is the best way to bring conformity.

Strong-arm Godlessness in the U.S.A.

That terror was brought home, literally, against one set of parents living in Ohio. In the fall of 2016, the state government forced these parents to give up custody of their 17-year-old daughter because they refused to accept her decision to become a boy and because they denied her opposite-sex hormone treatments.

The Christian parents (whose names were sealed in court records) objected on religious grounds both to calling their daughter by a male pronoun and to the state's decision to allow her to be transformed into a "male." The girl's state-appointed guardians not only took issue with these refusals, they also criticized the parents' decision to send their daughter to a Catholic school where the dress code required female clothing. In addition, they objected to the parents' decision to seek Christian counseling for the teenager and their requirement that she spend time listening to the Bible.

The parents' refusal to recognize their daughter's "maleness"—along with the Christian demands they placed upon her—made the daughter suicidal, state-appointed guardians argued to the Hamilton County Juvenile Court. The only way to ensure her safety, they concluded, was for the child to be removed from the home and to be allowed to have opposite-sex hormone treatments.

Bottom line: If a child complains that being required to live a Christian life makes him or her feel suicidal, then the state has a compelling interest (a legal right) to remove the child from the home.

This type of draconian action comes straight out of the Robespierre handbook of conformity through terror: It is "nothing more than speedy, severe and inflexible justice."

It is also a perfect example of what happens when the "world" of unbelievers is allowed to subdue the Earth while Christians sit back and wait on the wrath of God to address their problems and exact vengeance.

Stealing a daughter from the arms of loving parents who are simply trying to lead a Christian life—and who want to set an example for their offspring and impart those values to their children—is no small matter. Most would consider it a crime in and of itself.

A Biblical Tale of Kidnapping

In fact, the first recorded battle in the Bible ended up being fought over a similar issue—a family being ripped from their home.

The conflict is recorded in Genesis 14: 1-16 and is known as the War of the Nine Kings, which involved four northern kingdoms, in Mesopotamia, against five southern kingdoms in the Jordan plain. The northern forces overwhelmed the southern kings, killing many combatants while driving others into tar pits and into the mountains.

In the process, the northern kings captured the cities of Sodom and Gomorrah and took their goods, provisions and what remained of their citizens, including Lot, the nephew of Abram who would later become the father of the Israelites.

When Abram learned that his nephew had been taken prisoner, he gathered 318 trained men—all born in his household—and went in pursuit of the kings to the city of Dan. He deployed his troops at night and "brought back his relative Lot with his possessions, and also the women, and the people." (Gen. 14:16 NASB, emphasis added)

The northern kings could have justified their kidnapping of Lot and his family by simply claiming it was a rescue mission. Lot lived in a city of depravity. He was continually "vexed with the filthy conversation of the wicked" that he had to hear and witness every day in his hometown of Sodom. (2 Peter 2:7) The kings could have said Lot was suicidal and that it was in his best interest to be taken away. They could have added that Lot's children were living in an immoral climate, being exposed daily to wicked, grievous sin.

Abram's response would have been no different. He would have killed the kidnappers of his family members and gathered his loved ones back into his fold.

Vital Principles for the Christian Warrior

The past two chapters have examined important spiritual and human principals that the Christian warrior must understand.

Those who take up the sword to force their opinions and beliefs on others can only be *stopped* with a sword. Many governments in history have raised the sword against their own citizens, spurred on by a lack of fear of those citizens, and especially when those citizens live in fear of their leaders.

John Dickinson, author of the Declaration of 1775.

The early 20th century writer and publisher John Basil Barnhill best summarized this point when he wrote in 1914 (and many writers have wrongfully attributed this quote to Thomas Jefferson): "Where the people fear the government you have tyranny. Where the government fears the people you have liberty."

We know that God has not called us into fear. He has instead called us to "subdue" the Earth and to make it our bondservant. We are to subdue kingdoms, promote righteousness, make disciples of all men, obtain promises, stop the mouths of lions, quench the violence of fire, escape the edge of the sword and "turn to flight the armies of aliens."

The Greek word for "aliens" is allótrios, meaning "not one's own; an enemy; belonging to another." The Earth does not belong to these "aliens." It is not their birthright. It belongs to another; that is, it belongs to Christians as stewards of God's Earth.

Christians have not been placed on Earth to be the pawns or puppets of atheists, secularists, humanists, the godless or Muslims. We should reject any notion that we will ever be their bondservants or subdued by them. In fact it is *they*, in their attempts to gain the upper hand, who should fear *us*.

CHAPTER EIGHT:

GETTING TO KNOW THE ENEMY

Stand yourground. Don't fire unless fired upon. But if they mean to have a war, let it begin here.
(Capt. John Parker at Lexington Green, Mass., April 1775)

No one really knows who fired the first shot of the American Revolution, on April 19, 1775. It was also the start of the Battle of Lexington and Concord in Middlesex County, Mass.

Some have described the conflict as a brief skirmish; others say it was a bloody massacre. However it may be characterized, no one is disputing that it was the battle that started the war and saw eight American militiamen killed and one British soldier wounded.

Accounts vary on who actually fired first, with each side predictably blaming the other. For the purposes of this book it does not matter whether the British fired first or the Americans. What matters is that Captain John Parker ordered his troops of the Massachusetts Militia *not* to be the first to fire.

The Importance of Not Being the Aggressor

This is important, because from the start of America's rebellion the Patriots wanted to define the American Revolution as a war of self-defense. This, they believed, was in keeping with the Apostle Paul's instruction that Christians should obey authorities unless government has lost its ordained power to rule and has started attacking citizens.

Shortly after this initial battle, a declaration was drawn up by the United Colonies of North America to clarify that America was engaging Britain in a *defensive* war. More specifically, the declaration said the war was "in defence of freedom that is our birthright." It added that

Americans would take up arms to defend those freedoms until victory was theirs.

The colonies wanted the world to know that they were the defenders, not the aggressors, against a hostile British government: " … We have taken up arms. We shall lay them down when hostilities shall cease on the part of the aggressors, and all danger of their being renewed shall be removed, and not before," read the declaration of July 6, 1775, which was authored by John Dickinson and based on an earlier draft by Thomas Jefferson.

The framers obviously had Romans 13 in mind when they declared their intentions to take up arms in a *defensive* war.

The Apostle Paul admonishes all followers of Christ "to be subject to governing authorities." (v.1) But Paul goes on to describe some of the duties, expectations and limits to which the government must be subject.

Rulers, the Apostle said, must do good works and be ministers of good and only bring terror upon evil. Of vital importance, a ruler must be "God's minister" for good. (v.6) America's Founding Fathers believed that once the British government ceased to be a minister of good, it lost God's authority to rule and its citizens had an obligation to resist (not the same as taking up arms as an aggressor).

The Rev. Jonathan Mayhew examined Romans 13 in exacting detail in 1750 and delivered one of the most powerful sermons in American history. His conclusions on Romans 13 served as the Christian basis for many in the American Revolution.

"Common tyrants and public oppressors are not entitled to obedience from their subjects, by virtue of anything here laid down by the inspired apostle," the Rev. Mayhew said, referring to Apostle Paul's command that citizens obey civil authorities.

When government "becomes a common curse to society," Mayhew said, it is society's duty to "withhold from our rulers that obedience and subjection" that would ordinarily be rendered to them.

He added that when a ruler "turns tyrant, and makes his subjects his prey to devour and to destroy, instead of his charge to defend and cherish, we are bound to throw off our allegiance to him, and to resist."

Living under tyranny was absurd, Mayhew believed:

> *"Tyranny brings ignorance and brutality along with it. It degrades men from their just rank, into the class of brutes. It damps their spirits. It suppresses arts. It extinguishes every spark of noble ardor and generosity in the breasts of those who are enslaved by it ..."*

The laws of God—truth, equity and liberty—cannot be overturned by acts of government, Mayhew reasoned. He went on to ask what solution could possibly be acceptable other than "resistance to such a tyrant, by the name of rebellion?"

Even the British-supporting Rev. Jacob Duché agreed that this was the proper interpretation of Rom. 13:

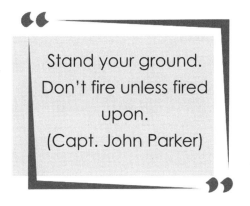

> *"Inasmuch as all rulers are in fact the servants of the public and appointed for no other purpose than to be 'a terror to evil-doers and a praise to them that do well,' whenever this Divine order is inverted—whenever these rulers abuse their sacred trust by unrighteous attempts to injure, oppress, and enslave those very persons from whom alone, under God, their power is derived—does not humanity, does not reason, does not Scripture, call upon the man, the citizen, the Christian of such a community to 'stand fast in that liberty wherewith Christ ... hath made them free!' " (Gal. 5:1)*

> *"The Apostle enjoins us to 'submit to every ordinance of man for the Lord's sake,' but surely a submission to the unrighteous ordinances of unrighteous men, cannot be 'for the Lord's sake,' for 'He loveth righteousness and His countenance beholds the things that are just.' "*

The colonists agreed, writing in their 1775 declaration that this was plain "common sense." Anyone who has a reverence for God knows, the document declares, "that government was instituted to promote the welfare of mankind, and ought to be administered for the attainment of that end."

The declaration made clear that citizens should not immediately take up arms against a government that has lost God's authority to rule. As such, the signers of the 1775 declaration pointed to numerous occasions when the colonies had previously sought redress for their grievances before taking up arms. They had offered several "humble and dutiful" petitions to the king. They had "pursued every temperate, every respectful measure" to persuade the king to stop trampling on their liberties.

The only option left, after the king repeatedly refused their requests and petitions, was for the colonies to stand their ground and resist British tyranny. Should that resistance be met with force, the colonists believed they had the God-given right to defend themselves.

Though the wording might be awkward to 21st-century Americans, it is worth rereading the declaration's ultimatum and warning to King George III:

> "... we most solemnly, before God and the world, declare, that, exerting the utmost energy of those powers, which our beneficent Creator hath graciously bestowed upon us, the arms we have been compelled by our enemies to assume, we will, in defiance of every hazard, with unabating firmness and perseverance, employ for the preservation of our liberties; being with one mind resolved to die freemen rather than to live slaves."

To put it simply, the declaration announced that the colonies were placing their rebellion before the eyes of God who would empower them and give them energy; that they were taking up arms only because the British government compelled them to; that they would remain firm in their defensive efforts in the face of every hazard; and that they would persevere until they either won back their liberties or were defeated—for they would rather die free than live in slavery.

The Rev. Dr. John Witherspoon, a signer of the Declaration of Independence, also affirmed that America's conflict with Britain was a defensive war:

"On the part of America, there was not the most distant thought of subverting the government or of hurting the interest of the people of Great Britain, but of defending their own privileges from unjust encroachment; there was not the least desire of withdrawing their allegiance from the common sovereign [King George III] till it became absolutely necessary—and indeed, it was his own choice." — The Works of John Witherspoon *(Edinburgh: J. Ogle, 1815), Vol. IX, p. 250, "The Druid," Number III.*

The authors of this book agree that this should be the standard and model of citizen and Christian resistance in America toward acts of tyranny, for this is what truly makes us American.

Government was created by God as a minister for good. When it ceases to promote good and stops honoring human liberties and freedoms, it loses its God-given authority to rule. All petitions and grievances should be delivered to ruling authorities first, of course, but if those complaints go unheeded and uncorrected, then citizens have a right to stand firm and resist. If government decides to use force to compel citizens into obedience, then citizens have the right to use force in their own defense.

To be abundantly clear, at no time do Christians—as followers of Christ or as citizens of America—have a right to take up arms against their government as the aggressor.

Captain John Parker followed this directive when he admonished his soldiers, "Stand your ground. Don't fire unless fired upon."

George Washington in 1777, a year after the war began, noted that "the Sword was the last Resort for the preservation of our Liberties." The "sword" should be the last resort for us as well.

War through Violent and Nonviolent Means

When we think of war we typically think of guns, bombs and other assorted weaponry. Yet there is much more to war than rolling out troops, tanks, machine guns and missiles for eliminating enemies. Make no mistake, though the colonists saw their share of British bullets, bayonets and cannon balls, they also faced less violent means used by the British to neuter their unruly subjects—that is, non-military weapons loaded for the demoralization, dehumanization and brutalization of patriot soldiers and civilians alike.

We should examine these strategies because they are part of the blueprint to oppress Christians in modern-day America.

It is important to understand that Britain did not want to go to war with the colonies. Britain was in debt from the Seven Years' War that had recently ended in 1763. Their overall standing army was relatively small, with regiments scattered in Ireland, Gibraltar, England and America, totaling a meager 45,000 men with just 10,000 stationed on American soil. Troop strength was so inadequate that Britain had to hire German mercenaries (the Hessians) to help with its American war efforts.

Besides being militarily unprepared for a fight that required English soldiers to sail roughly 3,000 nautical miles just to land in America, King George III hated the idea of making war against subjects he viewed as his beloved family members.

Modern biographer Stella Tillyard described King George III as believing he was America's "loving and tender father to young children and to his siblings as long as they remained dutiful and loyal … " (*Scars of Independence: America's Violent Birth,* Holger Hoock, 2017, Crown Publishing Group)

Because of this, England would introduce new elements into

This church directory in California was removed after objections from atheists.

warfare that were designed to divide and conquer the rebellious colonies rather than engage in the wholesale shedding of its distant family members' blood. This was made all the more possible, Britain anticipated, because they had loyalists in key positions in America—inside churches, newspapers, publishing houses, courts, schools and government offices. In this unique conflict, England could prosecute the war from both inside and outside the country.

England's blueprint for engaging with and defeating the American colonists can be summed up easily: It was a plan to bring the rebels into submission by terrorizing and dehumanizing the insurgents, torturing the captured, breaking the rebels financially, criminalizing their behavior, forcing them out of their homes and businesses, ostracizing them and isolating them from their loyalist neighbors.

Killing too many insurgents, England believed, was bad for publicity at home. Many Englishmen opposed the war and did not look kindly on the massacre of fellow citizens abroad. So the overriding goal was to demoralize the Yankees into submission, make the loyalists fearful about switching sides, and end the revolt using the bare minimum amount of soldiers and bullets.

Plunder, rape, burning farms and hanging traitors were part of the English strategy to bring the Patriots back into submission, but with the aid of local courts, Anglican churches, publications and sympathetic government officials they could also focus on defeating their enemy through less violent means. They would accuse the Patriots of false offenses, force them out of work, denigrate their ideas, attack them at public events, characterize them as being ignorant or inhuman, make them fearful to speak, outlaw town meetings, shut down courts, refuse to implement colonial laws and generally try to make them feel like a freakish and doomed minority.

Sound familiar?

It's Happening Again, Right Here and Now

Perhaps you have realized by now that the enemies of Christians in America are using similar tactics to defeat the Gospel message, God's truths and the Christian spirit. The effect of these strategies is to drive a deep, personal and unforgiving wedge between Christians

Evangelist Dr. Jerry Falwell took on pornographer Larry Flynt in the 1980s after Flynt defamed Dr. Falwell's mother in a profane spoof in *Hustler*.

holding conservative, traditional values and those who would rather live a godless existence, or at least an existence void of authentic Biblical truths.

Just as with the English strategy used in the American Revolution, the goal of God's enemies in the United States is to draw a clear line that forces Americans to choose sides. One side is portrayed as outdated, embarrassingly ignorant, repressive, hateful and even mentally ill; the other is relentlessly portrayed as progressive, compassionate, open-minded, fun, enlightened, accepting and generally "cool."

Since God's enemies are unable to use facts or truth to back up their negative portrait of Christians, they instead avoid real debate by using a grab bag of half-truths and outright fictions, false accusations, legal suppression, violence, mockery, destruction, indoctrination and name-calling.

Former Arkansas Governor and onetime presidential candidate Mike Huckabee explained it this way on FOX News:

"Today, the new direction of the left is: In the name of tolerance be intolerant. In the name of love, hate people. In the name of diversity, demand conformity. Because that's where we are. And it's not enough for them to say we disagree and I

wish this person would change his mind. Today, it's 'let's put them out of business.' Let's close their store. Let's not allow them to continue to operate a business. Let's damage them professionally. Let's hurt their brand. It's all about destroying the other side, rather than disagreeing with the other side. Today, it's let's destroy everyone who disagrees with me."

Not just "destroy" those who disagree with the liberal left, but destroy all visible signs of their religious faith as well.

God's enemies, in their hatred of Christianity, have been fighting the public display of crosses and nativity scenes, as well as protesting Christian-themed performances, monuments, dedications, ceremonies, prayers, books and declarations for the past half-century in America.

Even something as minor as a public road sign listing area churches was too much for leftists to tolerate in Coronado, Calif. The roadside church directory was removed after objections from an atheist group. There were no religious words on the road sign, just the names and locations of churches. Somehow even the public display of a church name is now seen as a violation of the U.S. Constitution.

A park bench honoring a teen killed in a hit-and-run accident was removed in Charlotte County, Va., because it contained the offensive words: "Children are a gift from the Lord. They are a reward from Him."

The 1988 film *The Last Temptation of Christ* depicted Jesus as struggling with sexual thoughts, and having never risen from the dead.

An Attempt to Bully into Silence

The goal is to eradicate all public recognition of a Judeo-Christian God in America.

The Christian and Hebrew God once proudly honored by our Founding Fathers is being replaced with atheism, Earth-worship, self-worship or even the Islamic god Allah. In a paradox that makes no sense whatsoever, children in public schools are told either God does not exist and that all human life evolved from apes, or that if there *is* a God, his name is Allah and he alone must be worshipped.

Those who disagree with these new alt-truths are immediately branded with derogatory names meant to dehumanize both the individual and the group. We have previously discussed such pejorative names, and how liberals label those with whom they disagree as racists, white supremacists, hatemongers or some type of trembling, fear-afflicted "phobe"—homophobe, Islamophobe, transphobe.

The National Rifle Association and its members have been branded as a "terrorist" organization on multiple occasions by powerful political pundits, lawmakers, and government officials and by at least one sitting governor, Gov. Dannel Malloy of Connecticut.

If Christians and like-minded conservatives aren't being called names, they are being attacked, beaten, shot. In some other nations, of course, they are being decapitated or blown up. Radical Islamists are notoriously willing to plunder, rape and murder to silence or convert their opponents.

The loss of Christians' and conservatives' very right to free speech is now a constant, nearly daily threat. We have already examined some occasions when destruction and violence were used at both university and public demonstrations to gag conservative speakers. We are also witnessing how police are becoming puppets controlled by atheists and liberal antagonists who want Christians arrested and jailed for preaching the gospel.

Famed Pastor Philip "Flip" Benham was arrested in Charlotte, N.C., in 2018. He was jailed for telling a woman at an abortion clinic that she was "dead in her sin" for supporting abortion. He was then charged with "communicating a death threat," a completely absurd charge. The irony seemed to escape police that only a short distance from where Pastor Benham was arrested, abortionists were doing more than making a "death threat"—they were actually killing children without any legal consequences.

Mockery: Childish But Effective

Nor are name-calling, arrests, imprisonment and the forced removal of Judeo-Christian imagery enough for God's enemies in this battle. Mockery of Christians is also a key weapon in the armory of Satan's little helpers.

Christians are constantly ridiculed and belittled in news, commentary and even dramas and sitcoms. Joy Behar, a host of the morning show *The View*, declared that Vice President Mike Pence suffered from "mental illness" for stating that Christ speaks to him.

One of the first religious figures ever to suffer such public humiliation was Dr. Jerry Falwell, for whom both authors of this book once worked. In 1988 the noxiously pornographic magazine *Hustler* ran a full-page spoof article on the world-renowned pastor that depicted Falwell as saying his first sexual experience was with his mother when he was drunk. "Mom looked better than a Baptist whore with a $100 donation," the magazine had Falwell saying. The spoof ended with Falwell claiming, "I always get sloshed before I go out to the pulpit. You don't think I could lay down all that bulls**t sober, do you?"

Rarely do the media or entertainment industries treat Christians as anything other than buffoons, prudes, simpletons, mindless lemmings, lunatics, wife beaters, child rapists and murderers, executioners and hypocrites, to name a few.

Not content with making Christians look ignorant and stupid, the media also want to assert that conservative Christians have the *actual* message of Christ all wrong. Such shows as Showtime's *Shameless* make the claim that Jesus was actually homosexual. A play performed in a Manchester, England church (yes, a church) portrayed Jesus as a transgender woman. A play performed in New York City, called *Corpus Christi*, also depicted Jesus and His Apostles as gay men.

Director Martin Scorsese, a notable trendsetter in the entertainment industry for abusing scripture, released a film in 1988 called *The*

Last Temptation of Christ. The film not only depicted Jesus as struggling with sexual thoughts, but also as having never risen from the dead.

Actress Jennifer Lawrence, who rose to recent fame in the *Hunger Games* movies, said Christians carrying crucifixes "may as well be [carrying] pitchforks."

Even saying you are a Christian in Hollywood is off-limits to many actors. Actor and director Kevin Sorbo, an outspoken Christian, told the *Gospel Herald*, "I don't know why in Hollywood you have to be fearful to say you are a Christian, but there's a lot of bashing of Christians going on over the last decade."

When Hillary Clinton famously spoke in her 2016 presidential campaign of a "basket of deplorables," who are "racist, sexist, homophobic, xenophobic, Islamophobic—you name it," she was referring quite directly to Christian, conservative Americans.

Much in the way England used falsehoods, intimidation, incarceration, legalistic maneuvers, fearmongering and name-calling to isolate and divide the colonies into loyalists or traitors, God's enemies in America are creating a similar divide, using the same tactics, to cause societal animosity and division between Christians and non-Christians.

So Who is the REAL Enemy?

As Christian warriors, what are we to do?

First we need to understand that the real enemy is not those who pass laws against Christians, or the police who throw us in jail, or the maniacs who attack, beat, scream and shoot at us, or the myriad non-believers who use the courts to eradicate all visual imagery of the Christian faith and restrict God-given liberties.

The real enemy is not those who depict Christians as backwoods hillbillies and gun-toting primates, or those who want Christian parents to either accept the latest sexual perversion or risk losing their children, or those who want to indoctrinate children into humanism, evolution or even Islam.

According to the Apostle Paul, these people are just actors carrying out "the wiles of the devil." (Eph. 6:2) Old Testament figures became very familiar with these wily characters who rose up to destroy the lives, communities and ministries of the God-fearing.

The "wiles of the devil" can be found throughout the Bible.

Joseph's brothers carried out the "wiles of the devil" when they conspired to kill their younger sibling by throwing him into a pit. Ultimately the older brothers changed their minds, settling on the slightly less heinous deed of selling him off as a slave for twenty shekels of silver (though Rueben only discovered this plan later). Joseph's troubles did not end there, however. He was subsequently falsely accused of rape and thrown into prison. More wiles.

The Hebrew slaves saw the "wiles of the devil" when Pharaoh ordered the Jews to drown their newborn sons in the Nile. King David saw these devilish wiles when Shimei, the son of Gera, pelted him with stones and called him a murderer and a scoundrel. And who would argue that King Saul was anything but a satanic puppet for constantly trying to hunt David to his death?

More than once, men of God had to go into hiding to avoid these dangerous rulers and antagonists. Jesus himself went into hiding when people picked up stones to throw at him. Moses fled, and went into hiding, after it was discovered that he killed an Egyptian who had been beating a Hebrew.

Escaping the "wiles of the devil" can sometimes mean just that: going into hiding.

Solomon twice notes the value of hiding, saying in Proverbs 27:12 "A prudent man sees evil and hides himself, the naïve proceed and pay the penalty," and in Proverbs 28:28 he says, "When the wicked rise, men hide themselves."

Many Puritans had to flee England in the 17th century due to their belief that the church should be purified from Catholic practices. At the time, such a belief was punishable by fines, arrests or even death. Interestingly, these Puritan Christians preferred to escape England rather than take up arms and defend their religious freedom. It was probably a wise choice.

When Isaac, the son of Abraham, was told by King Abimelech of Gerar to "go away from us, for you are much mightier than we," Isaac simply moved on. He could have stood his ground and fought, especially since he was mightier than the king. Instead, Isaac picked up his tent and went into a nearby valley and dug a well. He would learn this was not far enough; as the king's herdsman said, "The water is ours." He moved again, dug another well, but suffered the same result. He moved even farther and dug yet another well. This time there was no quarrel and Isaac declared, "now the Lord has made room for us." (Gen. 26:1-22)

Hiding and fleeing are not always possible, as was the case for Daniel, Shadrach, Meshach and Abednego.

Shadrach, Meshach and Abednego were thrown into a fiery furnace for paying no attention to Nebuchadnezzar's gods and the golden image he made. Daniel was thrown into a lion's den for violating an official decree that banned his praying to God.

Evil men and women exist, there is no doubt. The real enemy, though, is not one made of "flesh and blood," the Apostle Paul tells us. Instead, we are wrestling with "principalities, against powers, against the rulers of the darkness of this world, against spiritual wickedness in high places." (Eph. 6:12)

So what is a Christian to do? The Apostle Paul has the answer:

We need to put on the "whole armor of God, that ye may be able to stand against the wiles of the devil."

CHAPTER NINE:

TIME TO GEAR UP

The violent and the valiant are they which take heaven by force; cowards never won heaven.

(William Gurnall, 17th century Anglican clergyman, author of "Christian in Complete Armour")

It may be difficult to visualize Christians decked out in suits of heavy armor—with military grade helmets, breastplates, shields, swords and other combat equipment. Paul's description of the armored Christian calls to mind a Roman soldier marching off to meet Hannibal. This is in stark contrast to characterizations of the modern-age Christian, frequently portrayed as meek, nerdy, feeble and sissified, like the children of Ned Flanders on the cartoon *The Simpsons*. Today's prevailing notion of Christians would seem to have them collapsing under the weight of such heavy armor.

It brings to mind a poster I once saw slapped to a wall in a church hallway. It depicted a Christian man who was small, frail and wimpy holding the hand of a very tall, muscular-looking and forbidding nonbeliever and leading him into a church building. I found the poster nauseating.

Why, I wondered, do Christians insist on depicting themselves as weak and spindly human beings, mere antlike figures in front of the nonbelieving world or at best a kind of Mr. Rogers, if you will? Is our history not rich with warrior heroes—Moses, David, Samson, Joshua, Gideon, Joab, the New Testament apostles, not to mention Jesus Christ himself?

The Apostle Paul understood this and believed Christians should never project themselves as timid weaklings who are prone to fainting spells and panic attacks at the mere thought of a confrontation.

Instead, he expects us to suit up with the "whole armor of God" and go into battle fully prepared for victory.

Paul tells us God's armor includes a belt of truth, a breastplate of righteousness, shoes for the preparation of the gospel of peace, a shield of faith, a helmet of salvation and the sword of the spirit. This armor is designed to help Christians achieve victory in the evil day over the "wiles of the devil" and "having done all, to stand." (Eph. 6:13)

What is important to know about this armor is that every component is needed to achieve that victory.

So let us gear up. We have at our disposal:

The Belt of Truth

It is fitting that the belt of truth should be the first armor mentioned: a leather strap encircling the waist. The waist reveals all that we have consumed. It reflects what we have digested. In this spiritual analogy, the waist is a repository of the eternal truths we have absorbed from feeding on God's word.

Knowing the truths of God keeps us from being brainwashed and sinking into a cesspool of falsehoods that the liberal left is constantly keeping full for us. We are continually bombarded with such lies as: There is no God. If there was a God, he is now dead. There are no inherent differences between men and women. Individuals can freely determine their own sex and race. An unborn child is not yet a human with the right to live.

Homosexuality is normal and harmless behavior. Gay marriage

Rev. Gretta Vosper: "I don't believe in supernatural powers, or Heaven or Hell."

is equal to marriage. Sin and Satan do not exist.

Readers of this book might regard these untruths as hard to miss, but for many Christians that simply is not the case. Large numbers of Christians—and churches and denominations to boot—promote homosexuality and gay marriage as normal and even question the very existence of God.

The Rev. Gretta Vosper stood in the pulpit of her United Church of Canada and told her congregation, "I don't believe in supernatural powers, or Heaven or Hell." After she made this stunning announcement, many congregants told her that they, too, had their doubts about God's existence. According to *Vice News*, which published the story, "They carried on without God."

The Rev. John Shuck, a Presbyterian minister in Elizabethtown, Pa., also says he does not believe in God.

"God is a symbol of myth-making and not credible as a supernatural being or force," he told Charisma News. There is no "afterlife," and the "Bible is a human product," he added.

Megachurch Pastor Michael Walrond Jr. told his Harlem, N.Y., congregants that believing Jesus is the only way to heaven is "insanity."

"If you don't believe in Jesus you are going to Hell. That's insanity in many ways because that is not what Jesus even believes," he said.

There is even something called "Christian atheism" infiltrating churches. It consists of people who like the overall teachings of Christ but reject the idea that He is supernatural or has redemptive powers. Most Europeans would consider themselves Christian atheists.

According to Lifeway Research, an organization that "equips church leaders with insight," only 24 percent of Christians surveyed *in America* could agree with this statement: "Jesus Christ's death on the cross is the only sacrifice that could remove the penalty of my sin."

The answer to this survey question alone demonstrates the pitifully meager knowledge many Christians have of God's truths. They have belts made of cloth rather than of leather and metal.

In another shocking survey, conducted by the Barna Group and the Seed Company in 2018, it was revealed that less than half of American churchgoers are familiar with the "Great Commission," a term used to describe Jesus' call to evangelism found in Matt. 28:18-20.

The belt, in Paul's analogy, is *truth* positioned as the centerpiece of God's entire armor. Satan can easily distort our ideas of Christianity and what it means to be a Christian if we lack knowledge of the truth. We will in fact be rendered naked before our enemies.

"His truth shall be your shield and buckler." (Ps. 91:4)

A Breastplate of Righteousness

Knowing that you have right standing before God is critical to being a Christian warrior. When engaging the enemy, a lack of confidence that God is on your side, or feeling that you are too unworthy and sinful to be of any use to God, will diminish your ability to confront what Paul describes as the "wiles of the devil."

It is important to understand just what it means to be righteous. It has nothing to do with the sins, failings and struggles in your life. If it did, no one would ever qualify as being righteous before God.

The first account of anyone having righteousness before God can be found in Gen. 15:5-6. God told Abram to look toward the heavens and count the number of stars, promising him that if he could do so, "so shall your descendants be." Abram believed God and it was reckoned to him as righteousness. As a seal of that righteousness, God commanded Abram to be circumcised.

To fully appreciate the Apostle Paul's armor, this must be completely understood.

First came righteousness due to Abram's faith in God and then came circumcision as a seal of that righteousness. (Romans 4:11)

Being righteous before God has nothing to do with going to heaven. It means that you are right before God because you have faith and belief in His promises. Abram didn't need to perform any special act to earn that righteousness other than have faith in God's promise. Christ did not exist at the time of God's promise to Abram, so there was no redemption for sin available. Nevertheless, Abram still had right standing before God because of his faith.

This is why Paul makes a distinction between a "breastplate of righteousness" and a "helmet of salvation," which is mentioned as a separate piece of armor later on. These are not interchangeable pieces of armor.

Having a breastplate of righteousness when confronting God's enemies is imperative because the enemy will hurl accusations at you for the sole purpose of discrediting your integrity, morality, honesty, trustworthiness and honor.

They will dredge up past and current sins.

They will attempt to drive a wedge between the Christian and his or her brothers and sisters by pointing out flaws, indiscretions, and mistakes.

They will use exaggerations, lies and rumors to attack your dignity and competence.

Some accusations may be true. Some may not be. Some will be distorted, usually exaggerated. Their goal is to rip the heart out of the believer's chest and separate him from God, which is exactly why "righteousness" is depicted as a breastplate covering the heart.

None of us, by his own merit, is worthy to be right before God. We cannot attain such worthiness through anything we do. Because of our faith and belief in God, though, we are considered righteous before Him and *nothing* can ever separate us from Him or His love—neither persecution, famine, nakedness, danger or sword! (Rom. 8:35)

There is no question that the enemy will lash out with accusations, condemnations and spurious denunciations to marginalize Christians and expose them to public condemnation. Liberal activists, the media, "educators" and celebrities, to name just a few, will work for your demise. But the Apostle Paul asks, "Who will bring a charge against God's elect? Who is the one who justifies; who is the one who condemns?" (Rom. 8:34 NASB) The answer is: Only God justifies and condemns. It certainly is not these enemies of God.

Often, though, it will not feel that way when one is serving as a Christian warrior. I personally have been accused of being a white supremacist and a fascist (I am neither and act like neither). I have been accused of stirring up violence and vengefulness and even of inspiring others to commit murder. None of this is true. But like all other Christians, I have past sins and current struggles that cause me to fall short of the glory of God. I go into battle each day knowing that these lies and sins can—and will—be used as daggers to pierce my heart and kill my message and make me feel unworthy to be God's warrior.

This is why the breastplate of righteousness is so vital. You must know that regardless of your past and present sins and struggles you are right before God, "forgetting what lies behind and reaching forward to what lies ahead." (Phil. 3:13 NASB)

If only they with perfect, stainless lives could publicly promote and defend God's truths, then no one would qualify for the job. Sadly, even Christians rail against their brothers and sisters as soon as they discover a sin in those people's lives, even if that sin happened years or even decades ago.

Our breastplate of righteousness stands as a defense against anyone trying to destroy our ministry. Bear in mind this truth: "The gifts and the calling of God are irrevocable." (Rom. 11:29 NASB) No one, be they Christian or non-Christian, can take away your calling or gifts.

TAKE UP THE
Shield
OF
Faith
WITH WHICH YOU
WILL BE ABLE
TO EXTINGUISH ALL
THE FLAMING
ARROWS OF
THE EVIL
ONE...

Ephesians 6:16

Shoes of the Preparation of the Gospel of Peace

This has nothing to do with the actual preaching of the gospel, but rather with its defense. Remember that Paul is telling Christians to put on armor that will provide protection against the wiles of the devil. So each part of the battle gear should be viewed as an item needed for protection. The key word in the name of this piece of armor is "preparation." We must be *prepared* to *defend* the gospel of peace.

Paul makes this clear when he tells the church at Thessalonica that he is "set for the defense of the gospel." (Phi. 1:7) He is ready to answer any question, defend any scripture and uphold any doctrine in the face of any adversary. He warns that there are those who would "trouble you, and would pervert the gospel of Christ." (Gal. 1:7)

As discussed previously, Satan has sown the Kingdom of God

with weeds, those who want to distort the Holy Scriptures and reject their most fundamental teachings. We see this in daily assertions that homosexuality is healthy and normal, gay marriage equal to actual marriage, abortion is morally acceptable and without cost, the Trinity does not exist, non-Christians go to heaven, that there is no real difference between God and Allah. Such biblical distortions occur both outside and *inside* churches, on an ongoing basis.

Adherents of Islam, for example, claim theirs is the one true religion and that Allah is the one true God. Islam in fact finds its roots in the Judeo-Christian Bible. Muhammad said that Allah wanted to make corrections to these Holy Books because they are full of errors and he claimed that an angel named Gabriel appeared to him in a vision. Gabriel told him, Muhammad said, that the real "gospel" of salvation is a story of purification by doing good deeds—prayers, almsgiving, fasting and righteous living—which may or may not get you into heaven.

Interestingly, the Apostle Paul foretold such lies when he said, "But though we, or an angel from heaven, preach any other gospel unto you than that which we have preached unto you, let him be accursed." (Gal. 1:8) Take that Muhammad.

A warrior must be prepared to defend what he believes; otherwise that soldier will be susceptible to lies, propaganda and deception. Such was the case during World War II, for example, when many German soldiers and citizens alike were convinced that Jews, the physically handicapped, homosexuals and the mentally disabled were subhuman and worthy of actual extermination. This occurred even though nearly 100 percent of the German population claimed to be either Protestant (66 percent) or Catholic (33 percent). Quite obviously, the majority of these "Christians" of Germany did not have their feet shod with the preparation of the gospel of peace and failed to make a defense of the gospel message.

Not only do we need to know the truth (the belt), but we need to prepare ourselves to defend the truth (the shoes).

The words of the Apostle Peter are instructive here: "Always being ready to make a defense to everyone who asks you to give an account for the hope that is in you, yet with gentleness and reverence."

(1 Pet. 3:15 NASB) That is being prepared for the gospel of peace.

Bottom line: "Be on the alert, stand firm in the faith, act like men, be strong." (1 Cor. 16:13 NASB)

The Shield of Faith

We know where faith comes from:

"So then faith cometh by hearing, and hearing by the word of God." (Rom. 10:17)

And we know what faith is:

"Now faith is the substance of things hoped for, the evidence of things not seen." (Heb. 11:1)

Paul also tells us that faith is a shield that can quench the fiery darts of the wicked one. (Eph. 6:16) Above every other piece of equipment with which we gird ourselves, Paul says, the shield is the most important. Without it, the rest might as well be made of papier-mâché.

The rest of Paul's armor is found attached to the body itself—the helmet, breastplate, shoes and belt. A shield is something quite different. It is intended to protect the entire body. It is the first, mobile mechanism of defense that must be defeated before the other elements can be successfully attacked. Also, it is the only armor Paul specifically mentions as having a single, direct enemy: "the wicked one."

If Satan can break down our faith—make us feel hopeless, insignificant, worthless, confused, exasperated—it is easy pickings from then on to whittle away at our defense of truth, our relationship with God, our efforts to defend the Gospel.

We immediately picture the shield as something we hold, a heavy piece of equipment that must be swung from side to side and up and down with incredible, superhuman dexterity. The slightest error, the slightest hesitation could mean a fiery dart to the head or heart.

But … that is not the case. As God told Abram, "I am thy shield." (Gen. 15:1) King David stated, "The Lord is my strength and my shield." (Psa. 28:7)

The shield is God and it is not something we wield with our hand and forearm. It is an all-encompassing shield of protection of a Divine nature. It cloaks our entire human body, not just the outer flesh, but the mind, soul, spirit and emotions as well. We cannot see it, but we know it contains the substance of things hoped for—victory over Satan, his downfall under our feet, the knowledge that the gates of hell shall never pull us in.

To the Christian warrior, cracks in one's shield can be devastating. Satan and his army of principalities, powers, rulers and spiritual hosts have no other goal than to achieve complete victory over God's people and to win their capitulation. For Satan this is not a part-time job. He does not get depressed, sullen, lethargic, ambivalent or even frustrated about it. He is not a quitter and you can be sure he has no intention of surrendering. He will find any crack in your shield and exploit it to the fullest.

This battle is not for the faint-hearted. Yet we are all called into this confrontation from the moment we accept Jesus Christ into our lives, for we have been told that, "The God of peace will soon crush Satan under your feet." (Rom. 16:20 NASB)

Those are *your* feet being referred to, the feet of Christians. That is our goal—crushing Satan and freeing his captives. We have to do it while "fiery darts" are being launched directly at us.

Faith allows us to see victory despite outward signals and appearances of defeat. Who would have predicted, for instance, that after the death of their leader (Jesus Christ), eleven poor, uneducated and politically powerless men could turn that fallen leader into a revered household

Corey Johnson, an ISIS-inspired convert to Islam, slit the throat of a family friend.

name over the entire globe that gave birth to the most sought-after religion known to mankind.

That is faith in action—the substance of things hoped for, the evidence of things not seen.

The Helmet of Salvation

As mentioned earlier, the armor of salvation is different from that of righteousness. Righteousness makes us *right* before God. Salvation, however, is our gateway to heaven.

> *"For with the heart man believeth unto righteousness; and with the mouth confession is made unto salvation." (Rom. 10:10)*

Righteousness and salvation are clearly two different things.

Abram's righteousness was sealed through circumcision. For us, righteousness is sealed through the death and resurrection of Jesus Christ. Eternity is our hope, which gives us confidence and security even in the face of death—an ever-present possibility in every place on Earth.

This is no less true today than it was a thousand years ago. According to Open Doors USA, a nonprofit organization that focuses on persecuted Christians around the world, one in twelve Christians alive today now faces "high, very high or extreme persecution for their faith." As recently as between the years 2005 and 2015, 900,000 Christians were martyred, an average of 90,000 Christians each year. It is something you do not hear much about in the mainstream news media, and it is highly unlikely to be discussed even in church.

Through righteousness we know we are acceptable to God and no one can destroy His love for us—not with words, actions, violence or even the taking of our lives. With the helmet of salvation protecting us we know that even if the worst befalls us, we will rest in the loving arms of God and Jesus Christ for all of eternity.

It means a lot that this armor of salvation is on the head, protecting the whole head—eyes, nose, mouth, ears and brain. Regardless of what we see, hear, say, think or even inhale (think about the Christians in Syria who have been targeted with chemical weapons) we know that with the helmet of salvation there is nothing man can do to us.

> *"In God I have put my trust, I shall not be afraid. What can man do to me?" (Ps. 56:11 NASB)*

> *"Do not fear those who kill the body but are unable to kill the soul; but fear Him who is able to destroy both soul and body*

in hell." (Matt. 10:28 NASB)

Of course, we all hope and pray never to be placed in such situations. But as we know, many Christians and Jews already have been and still are.

The surest means of preventing such deadly encounters is to make sure society never plunges into a moral abyss, into total human corruption or paganism. Throughout history, the combination of man-made ideals, fabricated laws, godless social norms and false religions have steered society into direct and violent conflict with those who hold and cherish biblical beliefs. The story of Lot is an excellent example. The Sodomites wanted to rape Lot, possibly kill him, for trying to protect his male visitors from the city's violent sexual predators. The citizens of Sodom were far beyond any words of reason, respect or godliness. They wanted sex with God's holy angels, even if it meant killing Lot. Such environments lead straight into deadly encounters for the righteous.

The more society adopts falsehoods in place of God-given truths, the greater the risk to Christians and Jews—something both religions have painfully experienced in the past and are currently experiencing in lands where Muslims and Hindus dominate. Do not be misled: America—the land of ultimate religious tolerance—is no exception. The United States is currently witnessing an ever-growing and vitriolic hatred toward Christians, spurred on by secularists, humanists, atheists, relativists, agnostics and radicalized Muslims.

This was on display in 2018 In Jupiter, Fla.

Corey Johnson, a 17-year-old Muslim, watched an online video produced by the terror organization ISIS which told him to kill nonbelievers. After being invited to a sleepover at a friend's house in the gated community of BallenIsles Country Club, Johnson slit the throat of Jovanni Sierra, a friend of the family, while she slept. When the mother in the house heard Sierra's screams she went to investigate. Johnson was waiting for her at the top of the stairs and stabbed Elaine Simon a dozen times. When Simon's son, Dane Bancroft, ran to her aid and attempted to rescue his mother, Johnson attacked the 12-year-old and stabbed him 32 times. The young girl died, but the mother and son were rushed to the hospital where, miraculously, both were expected to recover.

The police report read: "In his statement, Johnson advised he stabbed the victims because of his Muslim faith."

Examples such as this are why Paul encouraged us to "take up the full armor of God, so that you will be able to resist in the evil day, and having done everything, to stand firm." (Eph. 6:13 NASB)

This is also why the Hebrews author praised the mighty men of God—David, Gideon, Samson and others—who through faith "quenched the violence of fire." Which brings us nicely to the final piece of God's armor for Christians.

The Sword of the Spirit

This is not a literal sword, of course. Paul identifies the sword as "the word of God." It is a sword that is keen for many reasons.

It is sharper than any human-made, two-edged sword and can pierce the division of soul and spirit, of joints and marrow, and can discern the thoughts and intentions of the heart. (Heb. 4:12)

It is useful for teaching, rebuking, correcting and training. (2 Tim. 3:16)

It gives both light and understanding to the naïve. (Ps. 119:130)

It is right and true. (Ps. 33:4)

It is Jesus Christ in the flesh. (John 1:14)

But what makes this sword really remarkable is that the word is already written into the hearts of man. When you speak the word of God to people, using this powerful sword, you do not need to convince them you are right. They know that you are right, whether they want you to be or not. The truth is already there, absolute and pristine, accusing or excusing their deeds.

> "For when the Gentiles, which have not the law, do by nature the things contained in the law, these, having not the law, are a law unto themselves: Which shew the **work of the law written in their hearts**, their conscience also bearing witness, and their thoughts the meanwhile accusing or else excusing one another ..." (Rom. 2:14-15, emphasis added)

Just as penicillin works by getting into the body and bursting deadly bacterial cell walls, the Word of God works by getting into the hearts of men and bursting their falsehoods and evil plans. It is sharp and surgical. It penetrates marrow and joints, spirit and soul. It exposes thoughts and intentions that are not in alignment with the Word of God.

For those who are simply naïve in their wayward thinking or wrongdoing, the Word of God gives light. It helps clarify the law already written in their hearts. For others, who are determined to reject the word of God, it brings out hatred, wrath, violence and evil. They would rather "work around" their sin than obey God's Word—figuring they can negate the effects of sin using science, medicine and medical procedures, or they can simply reinterpret God's Word to fit their own preferred behavior. They might, for example, say that since Jesus never personally and explicitly condemned homosexuality, gay sex must be okay.

There is little doubt that such willful refusal to walk according to God's Word and His salvation is leading a rapidly growing number of Americans into what sociologists now call "deaths of despair"— deaths by drug overdose, alcoholism, murder and suicide. Sin engenders depression, illness, psychosis and even death to those who let themselves be immersed in it. Sin breeds despair, hopelessness and, most fundamentally, separation from God. In 2017, U.S. hospital admissions for opioid overdoses increased by an astounding 30 percent over the previous year, with the young being hit hardest. It is impossible to find true happiness, peace and comfort without God, but drugs have unfortunately become the predominant way for people to ignore, forget, obscure or simply reject the Word written in their hearts.

When the sword of God is used to impart truth, you are thrusting Jesus Christ into the life of that individual. Jesus is the Word and that Word has power.

Pastor Julius Zant of St. Andrews Episcopal Church in Salisbury, Md. understood this when a gunman entered his house of worship in December of 2017. Pastor Zant said the attacker burst through his church doors during a Bible study and demanded cash and cell phones.

After one parishioner put her cell phone on the table, Pastor Zant stood up and said, "No, we're not having this. We're not doing this." He then walked over to the gunman and said, "Leave, in Jesus name."

The pastor said he immediately saw a change in the gunman's demeanor, as if "this wasn't the right thing for him to do," he told the *Christian Post*.

After backing off just a bit, the intruder again pressed the muzzle of the gun against the pastor's neck, saying, "I don't want to do this."

Then Pastor Zant told him, "Well, then don't do it. You don't have to do this."

At those words, the gunman left.

The courageous Pastor Zant showed how the Word of God cuts deeply into the heart of man. He also learned that other protection is needed as well, however. He immediately beefed up security at the church, started locking its doors and placed a guard at its entrance.

It is sad and disconcerting that churches, presumably the safest places on Earth, are now under such frequent attack even in America. In only the past few years, examples are plentiful.

Devin Kelly murdered 26 people and wounded 20 others at First Baptist Church in Sutherland Springs, Texas. Emanuel Samson killed a woman and wounded six others at the Burnette Chapel Church of Christ in Nashville. And who can forget the day Dylann Roof walked into the Emanuel African Methodist Episcopal Church in downtown Charleston, S.C. and shot nine worshippers to death.

Simply promoting pro-family values can inspire violence, as the Family Research Council learned when Floyd Corkins walked into FRC's Washington, D.C. headquarters in 2013 and shot a guard. Corkins said he was angry over the organization's biblical position on homosexuality.

The situation for churches has become so desperate that local and federal law enforcement agencies have begun hosting forums on how churches can protect themselves. Alabama state legislators even pushed a "Stand Your Ground" law for churches that would permit the use of "deadly physical force" against anyone who tries to physically attack or kidnap an attendee, including anyone attempting to gain unlawful entry into the church.

These attacks serve as reminders to us all to suit up daily with the armor of God to be prepared to fend off attacks both spiritual *and* physical.

In Summary:

The belt of truth keeps us from being swallowed up by the lies, illusions and faulty rationalizations of the world. The breastplate of righteousness affirms that God looks on us as being acceptable in His sight, regardless of the world's efforts to condemn us for any short-comings we may have. The shoes of the Gospel help us to be prepared to make a defense of the hope that is within us. The shield of faith allows us to see victory in spite of the outward appearance of defeat. The helmet of salvation is our guarantee that regardless of what happens to us, we will be redeemed into the arms of our Lord. Finally, the sword of the spirit allows us to cut deeply into the hearts of man, illuminating and freeing the Word of God that is already within them.

Then there is this final note. Paul concludes by saying:

> *"Praying always with all prayer and supplication in the Spirit, and watching thereunto with all perseverance and supplication for all saints." (Eph. 6:18)*

Prayer is the preparation we undertake before putting on our battle gear, with an eye towards being watchful. Who would risk going into battle and being blinded by the plans of the enemy? We must persevere too, Paul says. There are no quick and easy victories. We must pray continually for our brothers and sisters. The battlefield can be grueling and messy. It can be dangerous and lonely. It can be exhausting and frightening. There is not a soldier in the world who will tell you they do not want or need the support of their friends back home. Our prayers give our front-line Christian soldiers strength, hope and courage as they stand in the defense of the Gospel.

Every morning we must be prepared and dressed for action, lest the enemy devour us.

> *"Be sober, be vigilant; because your adversary the devil, as a roaring lion, walketh about, seeking who he may devour." (1 Pet. 5:8)*

An un-armored Christian will be an easy prey.

CHAPTER TEN:

THE REAL MEANING OF 'TURN THE OTHER CHEEK'

You have heard that it was said, 'An eye for an eye, and a tooth for a tooth.' But I say to you, do not resist an evil person; but whoever slaps you on your right cheek, turn the other to him also. If anyone wants to sue you and take your shirt, let him have your coat also.

(Matt. 5:38-50 NASB)

Bible commentators have many and varied interpretations of what Jesus may have meant in Matt. 5:38-40.

If the scripture is taken out of biblical context, an extreme interpretation could have Jesus saying, "Christians should do whatever an evil person wants, relinquish all possessions to that evil person, allow that evil person to physically harm their bodies and, if this isn't enough, refuse to hold that evil person accountable."

This sounds ridiculous, but not according to renowned 18th century Bible commentator Matthew Henry, who wrote: "The plain Instruction is, Suffer any injury that can be borne, for the sake of peace."

Henry, like many other Christian pacifists who have misinterpreted these verses, was profoundly and terribly wrong.

So what did Jesus mean? Or as the popular Christian adage states it: "What would Jesus do?" Fortunately, a path to the correct answer does exist.

After the arrest of Jesus in the Garden of Gethsemane, Jesus was taken before the high priest Annas and questioned about His teachings and disciples.

> " 'Why do you question Me?' Jesus asked Annas. 'Question those who have heard what I spoke to them; they know what I said.' " (John 18:21 NASB)

An official standing nearby felt Jesus was being insolent toward the high priest and had disrespected his position. He slapped Jesus in the face and asked, "Is this the way you answer the high priest?"

Jesus did not *physically* turn the other cheek for another slap, however. Instead, He stood His ground (this is important to remember). Jesus then fired back at his assailant, "If I said something wrong, testify as to what is wrong. But if I spoke the truth, why did you strike me?" (John 18:23 NIV)

Not only did Jesus not *physically* turn the other cheek, but He also chose not to slap the guard back and give him that "eye for an eye" retribution he probably deserved. Christ could even have executed a far more vengeful response.

"Or do you think that I cannot appeal to My Father, and He will at once put at My disposal more than twelve legions of angels?" Jesus told Simon Peter as He was being arrested. (Matt. 26:53 NASB)

Jesus did not seek revenge, but neither did he turn His head for another slap on the face.

After His brief hearing with Annas, Jesus was bound and sent to Caiaphas, where the scribes and elders had gathered. Jesus was mocked, blindfolded, tortured, insulted, beaten and slapped some more. During His trial, false witnesses came forward and Jesus was again questioned. When morning arrived the chief priests held a council and decided to put Jesus to death. He was bound again and taken to Pontius Pilate, who would ultimately agree to Jesus' execution.

Then comes this important scripture as it relates to our opening verses, Matt: 5:38-40:

"Then the soldiers of the governor took Jesus into the common hall, and gathered unto him the whole band of soldiers. And **they stripped him** ... " (Matt. 27:27, emphasis added) Eventually they would take away all His clothes, including His tunic.

In a painful, gut-wrenching series of horrible events, Jesus gave us insight into the interpretation of Matthew 5:38-40.

An Eye for an Eye

Jesus said that rather than react by taking an "eye for an eye" as a form of retribution, a person should *not* physically resist his tormentors who are suing him in court. Jesus could have asked His Father in Heaven to send 12 legions of angels to deliver Him out of His coming ordeal. He could have exacted immediate vengeance. Instead, He submitted Himself to the judicial system, corrupt and unfair as it was.

Slap in the Face

Jesus said to turn the other cheek if someone slaps you in the face. Turning the other cheek is symbolic for standing your ground, refusing to move, rejecting compromise. When Jesus was struck in the face, He did not physically turn the other cheek for his tormentor to slap Him again. He did stand His ground, verbally defending Himself, and questioned the legitimacy of the assault. He remained entrenched. He did not make any concessions and He continued to speak the truth.

Take Away Your Tunic

Jesus said if the evildoer tries to "take away your tunic, let him have your cloak also." Soon after Jesus was handed over to Roman soldiers He was stripped of all His clothes, which would happen again before He was crucified:

> *"Then the soldiers, when they had crucified Jesus, took His outer garments and made four parts, a part to every soldier and **also the tunic**; now the tunic was seamless, woven in one piece." (John 19:23 NASB, emphasis added)*

Standing your ground against evildoers is risky. Refusing to compromise is dangerous. Speaking the truth could cost you a lot more than you first thought it would. You could lose everything—

your tunic, your cloak, your family, your job, your friends, your home, even your life.

Many have recklessly distorted, misinterpreted and twisted Matt: 5:38-40 into a series of verses that advocate capitulation, self-sacrifice and surrender, especially by those who like to conceive of Jesus as some sort of long-haired, squeamish pacifist.

To Take Up the Cross

Instead, these verses are instructions on how we should take up the Cross. We do not back down from God's truths *no matter who slaps us* or what it might cost in the end.

> *"Then said Jesus unto his disciples, If any man will come after me, let him deny himself, and take up his cross, and follow me." (Matt. 16-24 NASB)*

Picking up the cross is not a "take-it-or-leave-it" situation for Christians, simply because those who do not take up the cross are not worthy of Christ.

> *"And he who does not take his cross and follow after Me **is not worthy** of Me." (Matt. 10:38 NASB, emphasis added)*

Just because a person is saved does not mean that person is taking up the cross. You can be a good disciple of Christ and still *not* take up the cross. Taking up the cross has nothing to do with the act of going to church, ministering to the needy, spreading the Gospel or preaching the truth.

Taking up the cross is the willingness to lose everything and risk harm if someone tries to stop one from performing one's Christian duties and ministries. One must be willing to sacrifice everything — from physical safety to loss of property to forfeiture of life itself, just like Jesus did when He took up the cross.

This is what Jesus meant by saying Christians are worthy only if they are willing to deny themselves and take up the cross. The Greek word for "worthy" in this verse is *axios*. It means having worth or value.

A Christian is still a Christian even if he does not take up the cross, but it is important to understand that this person has no real worth to Jesus. Christ will find no value in a person who is unable to

Kentucky County Clerk Kim Davis, with Arkansas Gov. Mike Huckabee, refused to sign same-same marriage licenses, saying it was tantamount to giving her personal approval to gay marriage.

stand resolute for God's truths (turn the other cheek) or unwilling to lose everything if ever confronted (to part with both tunic and cloak).

Jesus went to the cross because he spoke the truth, not because He was a follower of God, not because He led a disciplined life, not because He fed the hungry or helped the poor or healed the sick.

Jesus was convicted for committing blasphemy, for claiming to be "the Christ, the Son of the Blessed." (Mark 14:61 NASB)

Our Christian actions alone do not constitute taking up the cross. The cross is taken up when we stand firm against the many enemies of God who walk amongst us.

> *"For many walk, of whom I have told you often, and now tell you weeping, that they are the **enemies of the cross of Christ**." (Phil. 3:18, emphasis added)*

It is not by accident or omission that Paul does not call these adversaries "enemies of Christians," but rather "enemies **of the cross** of Christ."

These enemies could care less about Christians who are willing to fold, capitulate or shrink away from standing firm in the truth. Those who have taken up the cross of Christ, however, are a different matter.

These cross-bearing Christians are a threat, an annoyance, a thorn, even a dagger in the heart to their godless view of life and eternal truth.

The goal of these enemies is to turn everything upside down: *God didn't create mankind. Man evolved and created God. God didn't create people "male and female." People can be whatever gender they feel like being. God didn't create marriage just for a man and a woman. Marriage can be same-sex.*

As the Apostle Paul would tell the Roman church, they "changed the truth of God into a lie … " (Rom: 1:25) They do not want that lie exposed. They will do whatever they can to shut God's truth down — from violence to litigation to vengefulness.

Virtually every Bible commentator and scholar writing on the subject of Matt: 5:38-40 understands that these verses apply to how Christians should respond if brought before the legal system. Christ became the very example of how to apply these verses as He was brought before the corrupt legal charade of the Sanhedrin court.

So there is a distinction between how Christians should respond if subjected to the legal system as opposed to being confronted by evildoers *who want to take the law upon themselves* to hurt, rob, kill or deprive people of their God-given rights and liberties.

All people have the right to defend themselves and their loved ones from physical harm or property theft or damage at the hands of lawless evildoers. Although our response might be different when engaging a street thug as opposed to an officer of the court, the principal of taking up the cross remains: We are to stand our ground, dare them to take the clothes off our back and steal everything we own. We are not moving. We will remain steadfast. Our hands and feet will remain nailed to the cross of Christ.

Refuse to Back Down

In previous chapters we have discussed cases in which Christians have been taken to court for exercising their religious beliefs. There are many good examples of Christians in America who have taken up the cross in defense of their faith.

Christian baker Jack Phillips of Masterpiece Cakeshop in Lakewood, Colo. was put up against that cross when he refused to produce a wedding cake for the same-sex marriage of Charlie Craig and David Mullins in July 2012. Phillips cited his biblical objections to providing the cake, but the Colorado Division of Civil Rights sued Phillips claiming he was in violation of the state's anti-discrimination law.

On June 4, 2018 Phillips overwhelmingly won his case at the U.S. Supreme Court in a 7-2 decision. But he had barely pulled those nails out of his hands, on that cross, when the Colorado Division of Civil Rights sued him again just weeks later, on June 28. This time he was being taken to court because he refused to make a cake to celebrate the "transition" of Autumn Scardina, a Colorado attorney, from a man to a woman.

With the legal help of the Alliance Defending Freedom, which had successfully fought for him at the U.S. Supreme Court, Phillips went back to court. After another grueling eight months of legal wrangling, the Colorado Division of Civil Rights settled and dropped the case in March 2019—another victory for Phillips!

It did not mean Phillips was now able to easily climb down off that cross. The settlement allows the transgender Autumn Scardina to personally file suit against Phillips and Masterpiece Cakeshop.

Among the many more examples that could be cited, the case of County Clerk Kim Davis, in Kentucky, is particularly noteworthy.

Davis was elected as county clerk for Rowan County, Ky. on January 5, 2015. As part of the job she was required to personally sign all marriage certificates. A few months after taking office, the U.S. Supreme Court legalized same-sex marriage in the landmark case *Obergefell v. Hodges.*

Davis became a Christian in 2011 and, with the belief that the Bible should be taken literally, claimed that requiring her to sign marriage certificates of same-sex couples would be a violation of her religious conscience. She was boxed into a legal corner: *Either forfeit her religious beliefs and sign same-sex marriage certificates or face jail.* She decided the proper response was not to sign *any* marriage certificates— gay or otherwise.

Ultimately, a homosexual couple, David Ermold and David Moore, entered her office and filmed Davis rejecting their request for a signed marriage certificate.

Davis felt the act of signing the document would be tantamount to giving her *personal approval* of an act the Bible describes as sodomy.

Her refusal was not only filmed by the homosexual couple but was then posted on social media and went viral around the world.

Ermold and Moore could easily have gone to a different county clerk's office in Kentucky and received a signed marriage certificate from a willing clerk. Instead they targeted Davis.

"This case is not about these plaintiffs' desire to get married, the case is about [their] desire to force Kim Davis to approve and authorize their marriage in violation of her constitutionally protected religious beliefs," said Roger Gannam, the lawyer at Liberty Counsel who represented her.

Davis would say, "I never imagined a day like this would come, where I would be asked to violate a central teaching of Scripture and of Jesus Himself regarding marriage. To issue a marriage license which conflicts with God's definition of marriage, with my name affixed to the certificate, would violate my conscience."

Davis asked the governor of Kentucky to protect county clerks who have religious or moral objections to putting their names on the certificates. Gov. Steve Beshear refused her request.

There was more bad news for Davis when a federal court sided with the gay couple and ordered her to sign the marriage certificate. When she refused, the judge cited her for contempt and ordered that she be put in jail until she complied.

Davis spent the next five days in the Carter County Detention Center in Grayson, Ky. While she was in jail, deputy clerks in her office began signing marriage certificates in her absence. The judge eventually released Davis and also allowed her to go back to work after she agreed not interfere with other clerks signing marriage certificates.

Former presidential candidate Mike Huckabee commented that putting Davis in jail was part of the "criminalization of Christianity." Sen. Ted Cruz of Texas declared that Davis was a victim of "judicial tyranny."

In the end Davis was victorious, though her victory not surprisingly received very little media attention. In one of his first acts as the newly elected governor, Gov. Matt Bevin issued an executive order on November 6, 2015 removing clerks' names from state marriage licenses. In issuing the order Bevin said he wanted to protect the religious beliefs of officials who are opposed to gay marriage.

Even in victory, Davis' troubles were far from over.

The American Civil Liberties Union sued her for $233,000 in hopes of claiming legal fees. A court denied their request. Another couple sought to have the state investigate Davis for official misconduct, an offense punishable by up to a year in prison if Davis were found guilty. The state's attorney general, however, declined to investigate.

Nearly two years later, Davis would again be sued for not issuing a marriage license. This time it was a lawsuit brought by Mark Sevier, a graduate of Vanderbilt University, who objected to Davis' refusal to grant him a license to marry his laptop computer.

Davis would become the target of Hollywood ridicule and the butt of comedians' jokes. Television programs including the Emmy Awards poked fun at her. *The View*, a daytime talk show with an all-female cast, saw one of its guests, Michelle Collins, saying, "Have you seen the lady? I'm serious. She's a monster."

Author Lilith St. Augustine wrote a sleazy novel about her called *Kim Goes to Jail: An Erotic Story*. Davis was slammed on *Saturday Night Live* in a sketch called "God is a Boob Man." A gay activist organization paid to have a billboard on display in Davis' hometown that mocked her.

The national media would try to discredit Davis' Christian morality by reporting she has been married four times, always failing to mention that three of those marriages took place before she became a Christian.

At one point early in her ordeal, Davis got so many death threats she had to change her phone number.

"She's gotten death threats that people are going to come to the office, kill her and kill all of her staff," said Matt Staver, her lead attorney. "We've gotten death threats for the same thing, that we're going to be carried out in body bags. We've gotten death threats that we're going to have bullets in our heads."

Persecution in the Land of the Free

These examples are just a few among many that have unfolded recently in America. Far worse cases could be found in the horrific treatment of Christians in some other countries. Still, both the Phillips and Davis cases are illustrative of the abuse, threats, danger and potential ruin Christians may find themselves facing if they take a stand for God in America, the land of the free, the last place on Earth where someone's personal beliefs are supposed to bring condemnation, discrimination, abuse and actual imprisonment down on their heads.

Most frequently, we are only aware of the surface struggles these Christians must face. Being subjected to a lawsuit is a horrendous ordeal to go through. Though Phillips and Davis were both represented by Christian-advocacy law firms, therefore saving them the cost of legal fees, not everyone has such a blessing when facing a lawsuit. Attorneys' fees typically start at $250 an hour. When two attorneys are jointly

working on the case, that hourly rate can easily double or more.

When The Muslims of America brought a lawsuit against Christian Action Network, falsely accusing us of libeling them as terrorists in our book *Twilight in America*, the first month's legal bill was a whopping $70,000. We had spent nearly $150,000 when a judge eventually dismissed the case before it went to trial. Had the case actually gone forward, we would have easily spent between $750,000 and $1 million in legal expenses. It could have bankrupted us.

Very few people have the financial resources to defend themselves in court when evildoers assault them with lawsuits, and even the independently wealthy or those fortunate enough to secure the services of pro-bono legal firms might still face jail, death threats, public exposure and humiliation, multiple subsequent lawsuits and bankruptcy. Those subjected to lawsuits risk having all of their previous sins nationally exposed, and of losing their friends, reputations, business associates and employment. A person who dares to turn the other cheek and hold fast is also a prime target for multiple smear campaigns, media ridicule, bans and deactivations by the autocrats of social media, civil lawsuits and fines.

It is not a pretty picture. But taking up the cross—an icon of pain, torture, humiliation, personal loss and death—was never meant to be a bed-of-roses proposition. It is more like a bed of thorns or nails.

Nor do Christians have the option of declining this suffering. This would cause them to be deemed unworthy of Christ, which would be the opposite of everything for which the Christian Warrior stands.

Afraid? You are in Good Company

It would be natural to feel frightened, reluctant or unfit to go through such an experience. This is not an unusual reaction; perhaps it is even typical. When God appointed Moses to free the Israelites from Egyptian captivity, Moses told God, "Please send someone else." (Ex. 4:13 NIV)

When God asked Jonah to preach against the city of Nineveh because of its sin, "Jonah ran away from the Lord." (Jonah 1:3 NIV)

Out of fear of being nailed to a cross alongside Jesus, Simon Peter denied knowing Christ altogether "and began to call down curses, and he swore to them, 'I don't know the man!' " (Matt. 26:75 NIV)

Gideon questioned his own worthiness when God told him to, "Go in the strength you have and save Israel out of Midian's hand. Am I not sending you?" Gideon could not understand how God could possibly choose him, seeing that his "clan is the weakest in Manasseh, and I am the least in my family." (Judges 6:14-15) In essence he was asking God, "What strength? I don't have any strength."

We know how all these stories turned out. Despite their fear and reluctance, each of these figures would undertake what God asked and achieve tremendous success: The Israelites were freed from Egyptian slavery; Jonah's preaching saved the city of Nineveh; Simon Peter would become the rock on which Christ would build His church; and Gideon would crush the Midianites with just a handful of soldiers.

For the purpose of this chapter and the points we are making, Gideon might well be the perfect character. His story illustrates so exactly what we think, fear and doubt when we are asked to take up the cross.

Our first questions to God would probably be the same as Gideon's: "Why pick me? Who am I? Don't you see how weak I am? There are billions of people in the world; why would you put Your finger on me for this task?"

We would look doubtfully and critically at our lives and re-sources, our weaknesses, our sins, our lack of wisdom and innate ability and see nothing but impending failure.

Notice that God *did not dispute* Gideon's arguments. Gideon did come from the weakest (militarily) and least respectable clan and family in Manasseh. God simply ignored these deficiencies.

> *"And the LORD said unto him, Surely I will be with thee,*
> *and thou shalt smite the Midianites as one man."*
> *(Judges 6:16)*

Those Midianites were a ruthless people, forcing the Israelites to hide in dens and caves in the mountains. Whenever the Israelites would try to grow food, the Midianites would destroy their produce. There was not enough food for oxen, sheep or a donkey. The Midianites' numbers were also incalculable—like locusts and camels without number, the Bible tells us.

We learn that Gideon and his small band of 300 men would have to fight an enemy that was 130,000 strong.

No wonder Gideon wanted God to send him reassurance and asked for a sign—twice: once by asking that a fleece be *wet* on otherwise dry ground and next by asking that a fleece be *dry* on otherwise wet ground.

The odds were impossible for anyone or anything except a powerful God. All the earmarks of impending failure were there: the wrong man, from the wrong family, from the wrong tribe, leading an underwhelming army that could field only one man against every 416 enemy soldiers. They had to do it without donkeys or camels and with scarcely any food.

In the end, though, Gideon's army won the battle. They won because the enemy soldiers turned on each other, confused by Gideon's (God's) strategy of blowing trumpets, breaking pitchers and lighting torches in the night at the start of the battle.

Gideon's army looked and sounded bigger than what it actually was. The Midianites, along with the other nations in the valley with them, panicked and could not tell friend from foe.

"The Lord set every man's sword against his companion throughout the whole camp." (Judges 7:22)

Even if we are not fighting mighty military battles involving thousands of sword-wielding troops these days, definite parallels still exist between Gideon's story and what Jack Phillips and Kim Davis had to face and possibly what all of us, as Christian Warriors, might have to face.

Both Phillips and Davis were going up against government entities of the United States of America, which had virtually unlimited resources, wealth, manpower and lawyers at their disposal. Imagine if they had not had the help of Christian legal firms offering pro-bono services, and had been forced to fund their own legal defense on the wages of a baker in Colorado or a county clerk in Kentucky.

Both also had to cope with death threats, with Phillips reporting that even the lives of his wife and daughter were threatened. They had to face public ridicule. Anything in their pasts could be exposed if it would make them feel weaker, smaller, more insecure, more isolated. They would become the targets of media outrage and of liberal activists who would constantly assault their characters.

Surely both of these events were Gideon-type moments. The odds these people faced were, I daresay, even more lopsided than the one-to-416 matchup that Gideon's army had to face.

Yet they both won!

Don't Be Paralyzed by the Past

Surely one of the greatest obstacles we will face when taking up the cross is agonizing over our own deficiencies and not feeling qualified—or "Christian enough"—to take a stand for God. We will look at our past, even our very recent past, and rule out being anointed by God for the chosen task.

This is totally understandable, especially in the present climate when the slightest indiscretions or infractions (to say nothing of larger ones) are brought to public light no matter how long ago they occurred. Something that happened decades in the past—back in one's high school or college years—is now fair game to impugn a person's current character, position, credibility and qualifications.

No one has a perfect past, to the best knowledge of the authors of this book, with the single exception of Christ Jesus. We have *all* fallen short of the glory of God (Romans 3:23). No one is "perfect," even after being saved. Christians will make mistakes they regret, some more than others and with some mistakes more serious than others. There is no point listing all the terrible sins that even Christians may commit while still remaining loved and accepted by God, and without sacrificing their salvation or worthiness to take up the cross.

> *"For I am persuaded, that neither death, nor life, nor angels, nor principalities, nor powers, nor things present, nor things to come, nor height, nor depth, nor any other creature, shall be able to separate us from the love of God, which is in Christ Jesus our Lord." (Rom. 8:38-39)*

Christians who "fall" are still expected to take up the cross, otherwise they will be not worthy of Christ. A checkered past, even a most recent checkered past, is no excuse for throwing down the cross when called and refusing to take a stand for Christ.

What happened in the past—even if it was as recent as yesterday, or an hour ago, or even a minute ago—is wiped from God's book with repentance. As we press on to become like Christ we will stumble many times, sometimes with more serious consequences than others. But it is a goal we strive toward daily. The only way to reach that goal is to get over what just happened and push forward.

> *"Brethren, I count not myself to have apprehended: but this one thing I do, **forgetting those things which are behind, and reaching forth** unto those things which are before, I press toward the mark for the prize of the high calling of God in Christ Jesus." (Phil. 3:13-14, emphasis added)*

The Apostle Paul's admonition not to dwell on past mistakes while pressing forward is an echo of King David's perspective on how God views past sins.

> *"As far as the east is from the west, so far hath he removed our transgressions from us." (Ps. 103:12)*

If anyone had a record of terrible, absolutely evil past sins, it would be King David. David committed adultery with Bathsheba, had her husband, Uriah, murdered and refused to discipline his son Absalom, who raped his sister Tamar. Yet, though he suffered under the discipline of God for these sins, David remained King of the Israelites and was recognized in *The Acts of the Apostles* as loved by God.

> *"He raised up David to be their king, concerning whom He also testified and said, 'I have found David the son of Jesse, a man after my heart, **who will do all My will**.' " (Acts 13:22 NASB, emphasis added)*

Anyone reading the many biblical stories about King David will know that despite his sins, he remained committed to doing *all* the will of God. Imagine the public beating he would take if he were to take a stand for God—on *anything*—in today's world. And the blows would come not only from the media and other God-haters; they would come from within the church community as well.

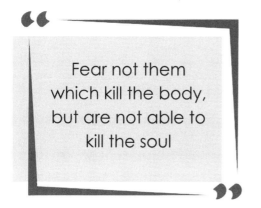

Fear not them which kill the body, but are not able to kill the soul

The Apostle Paul would not fare much better, having overseen the orchestrated murder of Stephen. Paul was known as Saul at the time and admitted to persecuting the church of God "beyond measure."

> *" 'And when the blood of Your witness Stephen was being shed, I also was standing by approving, and watching out for the coats of those who were slaying him.' " (Acts 22:20 NASB)*

> *" 'For you have heard of my former manner of life in Judaism, how I used to persecute the church of God beyond measure and tried to destroy it.' " (Gal. 1:13 NASB)*

Today, it is unlikely anyone would be able to have a church ministry, run for public office, become a judge or even head a corporate business with murder or violent religious persecution in their background, regardless of repentance. Changing one's name (such as from

Saul to Paul) would not be enough. These new societal norms are not how God looks at things, however. A person never loses God's calling.

"For the gifts and the calling of God are irrevocable." (Rom. 11:29 NASB)

God will not revoke a Christian's calling, for any reason. For some Christians this statement might be repugnant; they view the mere commission of these huge, horrible and tragic sins as cause for immediate forfeiture of any calling God might have had for that person. Those who hold such views have missed the point of Jesus' forgiveness, as told in the story of the woman caught in the very act of adultery:

"He that is without sin among you, let him first cast a stone at her," Jesus said in John 8:7.

No one is without sin, and someone else's is no greater than yours.

"For whosoever shall keep the whole law, and yet offend in one point, he is guilty of all." (James 2:10)

If you are guilty of lying, you are as guilty of sin as if you had committed murder or adultery.

These scriptures and examples show that we are all on the same playing field when it comes to taking up the cross. Personal indiscretions, bad habits, failings or lapses in judgment cannot be used to disqualify oneself from taking up the cross of Christ when the moment comes. Otherwise, no one would be able to step forward.

"If thou, LORD, shouldest mark iniquities, O Lord, who shall stand?" (Ps. 130:3)

This is not to say that Christians don't need to be ever mindful of their words and conduct. An unsavory, less-than-Christian lifestyle can make all a person's gifts and callings less effective in that person's outreach.

"Whether, then, you eat or drink or whatever you do, do all to the glory of God. Give no offense either to Jews or to Greeks or to the church of God." (1 Cor. 10:31-32 NASB)

Taking a stand for God's truths even when besieged by evildoers who have the ability to hurt you, have you thrown in jail, take all your possessions, expose your past, hold you up for public ridicule, destroy your livelihood and shatter life as you know it does bear a definite reward, and the Bible is very clear on this:

*"Blessed is a man who perseveres under trial; for once he has been approved, **he will receive the crown of life**, which the Lord has promised to those who love Him." (James 1:12 NASB, emphasis added)*

This "crown of life" reward for standing firm while under trial is also mentioned in Revelation 2:10:

" 'Do not fear what you are about to suffer. Behold, the devil is about to cast some of you into prison, so that you will be tested, and you will have tribulation for ten days. Be faithful until death, and I will give you the crown of life.' " (Rev. 2:10 NASB)

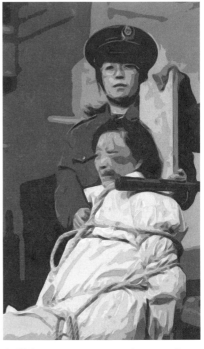

A Chinese woman undergoes torture for being a Christian.

The Crown of Life is not something bestowed on an individual for accepting Christ and attaining salvation. It is rather one of five crowns mentioned in the Bible that are given only as rewards for certain achievements. The other four crowns are: The Imperishable Crown, the Crown of Righteousness, the Crown of Glory and the Crown of Rejoicing.

The Crown of Life is gained by persevering under trial even to the point of going to prison and even facing death. To be clear, going to prison and becoming a martyr are not requirements for receiving the Crown of Life. It is the willingness to face that testing, even to the point of suffering jail and/or execution, that earns the reward.

Our goal is to defend the Kingdom of God, which is here and now and all around us. The Kingdom is not something that comes out of heaven in some far-off distant future when Jesus returns. It is not going to be something you can point to or show to people.

Jesus said, "Nor will they say, 'Look, here it is!' or, 'There it is!' For behold, **the kingdom of God is in your midst."** (Luke 17:21

NASB, emphasis added) And, "From the days of John the Baptist **until now** the kingdom of heaven suffers violence, and violent men take it by force." (Matt. 11:12 NASB, emphasis added)

We have been chosen to be soldiers of Christ because the Kingdom will suffer violence. (2 Tim. 2:4) Like the brave soldiers who risk their lives in defense of our country every day—protecting our values and beliefs along with our land and property—we stand as good soldiers ready to suffer in defense of the Kingdom of God.

"Join with me in suffering, like a good soldier of Christ Jesus," Paul told Timothy (2 Tim. 2:3 NIV).

A soldier does not go into battle unprepared and neither should we. The Apostle Peter tells us we should "always be prepared" to offer defense for our faith and to do it with "meekness and fear." (1 Pet. 3:15)

The Greek word for "fear" in this verse is *phobas*, which means to strike terror. It *does not* mean that we should fear evildoers. Jesus tells us, "fear not them which kill the body, but are not able to kill the soul." (Matt. 10:28) Neither does it mean evildoers should fear us. We should present ourselves as meek and humble.

What evildoers should "fear" is the Lord, when we answer them and give a defense for the "hope that is within us." Though the "wages of sin is death," we must also convey God's love. Having this "fear" of the Lord means not only fearing God's wrath, but also gaining His rewards.

The Bible tells us that those who "fear" the Lord are blessed with mercy, instruction, no want, lovingkindness, His shield, favor, salvation, wisdom and knowledge. (Luke 1:50; Ps. 27:12, 34:9, 103:11, 115:11, 147:11; Isaiah 33:6)

There is no question that the Apostle Peter is instructing us how to respond in an arena entirely different from that of typical evangelism. This arena involves making a "defense" of God's truths. It has nothing to do with voluntarily sharing the Gospel, but rather how to respond when required to give an answer for "the hope that is in you" to an opponent.

The Apostle Paul says to Timothy:

" 'Opponents must be gently instructed, in the hope that

> God will grant them repentance leading them to a knowledge
> of the truth, and that they will come to their senses and es-
> cape from the trap of the devil, who has taken them captive to
> do his will.' " (2 Tim. 2:6, NIV)

But not all "opponents" will heed this good news and truth, or fear God at the end. Therefore, we must be prepared to suffer as good soldiers in Christ:

> "Then shall they deliver you up to be afflicted, and shall kill
> you: and ye shall be hated of all nations for my name's sake."
> (Matt. 24:9)

Sometimes offering no answer at all to your opponent is the proper response. Jesus continually frustrated His inquisitors by refusing to respond to harsh accusations made against Him.

> "Then Pilate questioned Him again, saying, 'Do You not
> answer? See how many charges they bring against You!'
> But Jesus made no further answer; so Pilate was amazed."
> (Mark 15:4-5 NASB)

Jesus also frustrated the high priest Annas when He refused to answer the false charge that He would destroy the temple and make another one without the use of hands:

> " 'Do You not answer? What is it that these men are testify-
> ing against You?' But He kept silent and did not answer."
> (Mark 14:60 NASB)

Jesus knew that at times it is pointless, even harmful, to argue with these enemies of the cross and He warned us not to engage with them:

> "Do not give what is holy to dogs, and do not throw your
> pearls before swine, or they will trample them under their
> feet, and turn and tear you to pieces." (Matt. 7:6 NASB)

These dogs, these swine cannot be persuaded by reason or scripture. Their sole purpose is to trample your arguments (pearls) under their feet and tear you apart. It is one thing to argue with an evildoer—even an evildoer who is trying to have you put in jail—if that enemy can be persuaded by your defense. It is another to cast Christ's "pearls" before those whose sole goal is to make a public mockery of those riches and trample the Word of God down into the mud.

The reasons why Christians have turned to martyrdom are many and varied. John the Baptist was beheaded because he told King Herod it was unlawful to have his brother's wife. Stephen was stoned to death (as told in Acts 7) because he proclaimed that he saw Jesus standing at the right hand of God. King Herod killed the Apostle James with a sword because Herod derived pleasure from killing a Christian.

Christians have been murdered for the amusement of others, for politics, for refusing to recant their beliefs and for failing to mold themselves to societal expectations. Muslims have killed Christians simply because they were Christians, while so-called Christians have killed other Christians over doctrinal disputes.

In 2019, the Chinese communist government promised to rid its society of Christian, "western" influence by arresting and jailing Christians and rewriting the Bible to include Buddhist scripture and Confucian teachings.

From the time of Christ to current times, the Kingdom of God has suffered and still suffers great violence.

What these martyred Christians had in common was their willingness, as exemplified by Jesus Christ, to turn the other cheek (stand their ground) and sacrifice all their earthly possessions (losing both tunic and cloak) to defend the hope that was within them.

The Christian Warrior must be willing to take up that cross, if he or she wants to have any worth to Christ. It does not sound fun, desirable or inviting. We logically and naturally fear the pain, suffering and agony of going to jail or becoming a martyr.

Bestselling author Amy Welborn writes about the thousands of martyrs whose executions were meant to be painful:

> "But the strange thing is, the stories that come down to us about their deaths, even those few stories recorded by the Romans who killed them, tell us that most of these women, men, and children who were killed for their faith died with peaceful hearts, sometimes even singing hymns as they were burned or dragged by animals in front of the cheering crowds." (Book of Heroes, Loyola Press, 2003)

There are notable examples of Christian martyrs enduring the pain of execution, beyond the biblical story of Stephen whose face shown like an angel's as he was being stoned to death.

St. Sebastian was condemned to death in 288 A.D. for the criminal act of converting Roman soldiers to Christianity. He was taken to a field, tied to a stake and shot by archers until he was filled with arrows and presumed dead. He was not dead, however, and was nursed back to health by a woman who went to retrieve his body. Undeterred by the pain and suffering of his near-death experience, Sebastian went to a staircase where the emperor was about to descend and berated him for his cruelties to Christians. Sebastian was then clubbed to death and thrown into a Roman sewer, having been willing to take up the cross not once but twice!

St. Lawrence, one of the most venerated saints of the Roman Catholic Church, was roasted on a gridiron over hot coals in 258 A.D. for giving material goods to church members. After enduring the agony for quite some time, he reportedly said, "I'm quite well done on this side. Turn me over!"

Perhaps most remarkable is the story of St. Catherine of Alexandria, who also ran afoul of a Roman emperor by chastising him for his cruelty to Christians in 287 A.D. Emperor Maxentius ordered the young girl, aged around 17 or 18, to be scourged. Her whole body was covered with stripes and blood poured off her. Spectators cried at the sight of her torture, but Catherine kept her eyes raised toward heaven and showed no signs of pain, suffering or fear.

She was then imprisoned without food. The emperor sent pagans to her jail cell to try and persuade her to recant her faith. The effort backfired, however; many of the pagans came away as converts to Christianity. All who converted were summarily killed.

The desperate emperor then ordered Catherine to be executed on a spiked wheel designed to break all her bones. But as soon as it touched her body, the wheel shattered. The emperor finally conceded that torturing Catherine was futile, so he had her beheaded.

More recent is the 2019 testimony of an Iraqi Christian who related a miraculous story of survival in the documentary film, *Heart and Hands: Iraq.*

The Yazidi man said armed ISIS fighters commanded him to denounce Christianity and accept Islam under penalty of death if he refused. When he refused to deny Christ, they stoned him. "They were hitting me with big rocks on my body," he said. "The stones were fine, not affecting me."

When that attempt at torture failed to force him to convert, he was drenched in gasoline and set afire. That too failed. Twice more ISIS thugs attempted to burn him alive, but to no avail.

"And they burned me, but I didn't burning," he said, and gave credit to Jesus for his survival.

Modern historians discount all these stories of executions intertwined with miracles, but they make Jesus' exhortation in Matthew 5:11-12 (NASB) much more comforting, meaningful and powerful:

> *"Blessed are you when people insult you and persecute you, and falsely say all kinds of evil against you because of Me. Rejoice and be glad, for your reward in heaven is great; for in the same way they persecuted the prophets who were before you."*

CHAPTER ELEVEN:

A VISION OF THE STRUGGLE TO COME

When the last days come, I will give my Spirit to everyone. Your sons and daughters will prophesy. Your young men will see visions, and your old men will have dreams.

(Acts 2:17, CEV)

Say or think what you like about dreams. Some people think of them as supernatural, prophetic or borderline miraculous; others see them as the random, nonsensical byproducts of sleeping but still busy brains.

As I age into my mid-60s, I certainly do not see myself as a young man having "visions." But I am certainly old enough (or is it young enough) to have dreams with a significance that is sometimes striking.

While writing these latter chapters I had one such dream. It came to me the night after our annual board meeting for Christian Action Network. During that meeting I suggested to the Board of Directors the idea of producing a film exposing the current radical agenda of the homosexual movement.

I proposed naming the film *Stolen Rainbow.*

God did, after all, create the rainbow as an "everlasting covenant between God and every living creature of all flesh that is upon the earth." (Gen. 9:16) It has always served as a visual symbol of God's creation of life and His love for humankind.

Militant homosexuals have stolen the imagery of that rainbow, however, just as they have hijacked such words as "gay" and "pride," to promote a lifestyle of debauchery, self-delusion and isolation. Perhaps most tragic of all, they have re-forged the rainbow into a weapon against God's gifts of sex, marriage, masculinity, femininity, gender, and all the good that comes from male and female distinctions.

Normally when I awaken from dreams I am left with only a few hazy, short-lived images of what I saw. Not after this dream. This dream was long, detailed, vivid, coherent, persistent—and disturbing.

Upon awakening from it I immediately began writing it down. As I wrote, God provided interpretations for each of my visuals.

First I will describe the dream. Then I will proceed to give its interpretation as revealed to me by God.

A Great Wave

It started with a huge, dirty and terrifying wave coming across an open land. People were running for their lives in terrible confusion about where the roaring mountain of water had come from, since there was no ocean or river nearby.

After the wave came a great lake of swirling, cresting and muddy water that was producing more tremendous and horrifying waves. Some people were in awe of it, sitting on the verge of a cliff looking down as the wild water kept crashing below them. Though the sight was terrifying to those sitting on the bluff, fleeing did not seem to enter their minds. Given their perceived degree of safety, they were more focused on watching the wondrous and cataclysmic waves

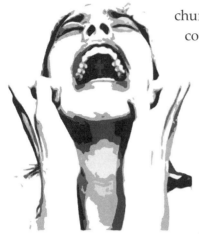

Despair is rampant throughout the world, the result of society's promotion of, and glorification of, sin

churning up muck than with seeking cover. Seeming unconcerned and even callous toward those below who were being swallowed up by the waters, some even perched on lawn chairs as they surveyed the cruel spectacle below.

Then I was running into a friend's house and asking him, "Do you see these horrible waves coming at us?" The friend said he did not. He looked out the window, though, and was immediately struck with bewilderment and horror at the tsunami-like torrent.

Outside again, with my eyes refocused on the lofty cliff spectators, I saw a huge and most dreadful wave rise out of the lake to roll straight toward them. It looked dark and ghastly and rose high as a mountain in the sky. This wave was also different in that it had two fiery red eyes in the center of its crest. The cliff spectators quickly realized these were the eyes of an angry God. They waved wildly at it, as if trying to appease their Maker before being overwhelmed. It did not help. The wave crashed against the cliff like an exploding bomb and shattered it, and the rocks and rubble all crumbled down into the dirty torrent intermingled with the heads and tangled limbs and chairs of the formerly lofty—and now drowning—spectators.

Bonnie (my wife) and I got into a car to flee the deadly waves. Bonnie took the wheel and we were almost immediately enveloped in a huge cloud of smoke that was impossible to see through. She was driving as if blind. She could not even see the lines on the road much less any cars that might have been in front of us. But this smoke cloud did not last long; we emerged from it in a matter of seconds. Now we encountered police officers stopping people before directing them to safety.

When we arrived at an area away from the chaos that appeared to be a safe haven, I felt we were somewhat free of the danger of what appeared to be some sort of judgment from God. For some reason, however, I felt compelled to try and raise funds for our film *Stolen Rainbow*. In the manner of dreams it all seemed a bit foolish and incoherent—a weird conglomeration of wild fantasy with my own real-life concerns. And anyway, I remember thinking, God's judgment was already upon the Earth! Right now! What good would it do? The fury of God was already upon us. Wouldn't this be a colossal waste of time?

Though it seemed pointless, I was consumed by the compulsion to start the film anyway. Perhaps there was still time. Who was I to decide? The last vivid emotion of my dream involved my effort to round up people to help produce the film.

The Interpretation:

As I mentioned earlier, after waking I decided to write down the dream. While I did so, God revealed the different meanings behind the events and images.

The muddy, foul and raging waters represented the current corruption of a sin-filled Earth. This explains the lack of an ocean or even river nearby, which drives home the fact that this terrifying torrent of pollution was created by man's own ruinous decisions—it his sin becoming fully grown.

The people unsuccessfully fleeing these waves were everyday people suffering, dying or being maimed by these tidal waves of corruption. The people on the cliff represented world leaders, activists and avowed promoters of the corruption filling the water. The fiery red eyes represented God's anger at the putrid water that man, himself, had created.

The people on the cliff were amazed at the destruction occurring before their eyes. At first they appeared unwilling to accept that it came from God or even that they had had any role in creating it. As the destruction ebbed and flowed, receded and resurged, they felt safe from its destructive power and showed contempt for the people below who were dying and suffering in the waves of corruption. When they finally saw the awesome and colossal wave with its fiery red eyes approaching their own position, they recognized God's anger. Realizing their impending doom, they desperately tried to appease God with friendly gestures. But, not knowing the way to salvation, they plunged into the deadly filth of their own creation. They were the enemies of God.

The friend whose house I entered, who did not even see the waves approaching outside, represented Christians who are oblivious to the corruption filling the world; that is, Christians who go about their daily lives not aware—perhaps on purpose—of the crushing waves of decay and destruction right outside their doors.

The detail of Bonnie being the one to drive the car as we fled (rather than myself) served the purpose of keeping the dream in the third person narrative. Bonnie represented all Christians who will seek safety from the corruption and death that is overwhelming the Earth.

The thick, visually impenetrable cloud of smoke on the road symbolized how Christians will feel blinded as they try to escape annihilation along with the rest of humankind. They will not see a clear path to safety, nor will they know what is immediately in front of them. They will fear the unknown that lies ahead.

The police officers just beyond the thick but short-lived cloud screen represented God's checkpoint for Christians who seek out and receive His guidance.

My search for funds to continue our *Stolen Rainbow* film was God's instruction that Christians should not simply give up on the world, halt their ministries, become fatalistic, surrender to the notion that all is lost. It was nothing less than an instruction against the sin of despair. We are to continue our mission of being "the salt of the Earth" and "a light" to the world even while facing the terrifying specter of self-inflicted doom.

Waves of Corruption

Whether my dream foretells the coming wrath of God or the natural consequences of compounding sin does not matter. It depicts calamitous events that await humankind for having abandoned God's truths in favor of lies, distortions, deceit and ungodliness.

Throughout most of the world God's truths have been polluted, poisoned, strangled and bastardized. The rejection of God's Holy Word has become so rampant that the world is becoming a truly terrifying place. In an article titled "Godlessness is Reaching Epic Proportions," published March 20, 2019, by the *Christian Post*, author Howard Green stated:

> *"Babies are aborted, children are discarded, and women are abused. Marriages are crumbling in record numbers and families are disintegrating because of sin and selfishness ... People don't just kill for cars, now they kill for parking spaces. People will walk up to complete strangers and knock them out for the 'fun of it.' "*

Many more examples could be added to Green's short inventory of humankind's self-destructive behavior. In skyrocketing numbers people are committing suicide, overdosing on drugs, contracting virulent and deadly STDs, being sexually exploited and abused and becoming the victims of patricide (killing of parents), fratricide (killing of a brother or sister) and filicide (killing of one's own offspring).

Lunatic gunmen are picking off young people (often their own peers) in the halls of their schools, or shooting people at concerts, clubs and sporting events. Even people strolling along city sidewalks with their families could suddenly be struck and run down by a deranged terrorist in a rented truck, who then gets out and sets upon his victims with a knife.

The mounting deaths do not come merely at the hands of bloodthirsty sociopaths. Every day people are dying internally from mental disorders, depression, hopelessness and anxiety.

Let's call it what it is: despair.

The number of young people going to emergency rooms in the United States with psychiatric problems jumped 54 percent from 2011 to 2015, according to a 2019 study by the Kennedy Krieger Institute at Johns Hopkins University in Baltimore. Suicide rates have more than doubled during that same time, the same study found. Deaths from the powerful opiate fentanyl rose more than 1,000 percent between 2011 and 2016. Syphilis rates for women in the United States nearly doubled between 2013 and 2017, according to the Centers for Disease Control. Since the outbreak of AIDS nearly a million Americans have died from the disease. Some 36 million worldwide are now living with the HIV virus.

Statistics can be dull and not too easy to digest, but a couple more need to be mentioned. According to the FBI, an American is now being arrested every 20 seconds for a drug law violation. Some 10 million people are currently living in U.S. prisons with another four million on probation. In 1920, the number of U.S. prisoners was a meager 250,000. Now nearly half of adults have seen a family member go to jail.

Cliff Dwellers

Like undersea earthquakes and landslides, sin can bring about waves of death, sickness, personality disorders, incarceration, isolation, poverty, disfigurement, disease and homelessness. The more sin pollutes our society, the filthier and larger those waves of loss, tragedy and disability become.

By permitting and even promoting sin, we are killing ourselves and destroying all we have. Hence the toxic and crushing waves I witnessed in my dream.

Mankind is born in sin and we are perfectly capable of being blinded to the muddy and dangerous waters threatening our lives and happiness. There are others, however—people we call rulers, advocates, influencers and experts—who use their power, charisma, humor, beauty and quick wits to lead others squarely into the muddy waters. Not content to darken only their own lives, they feel a desperate need to spread and promote their self-destructive lifestyles to others. They legalize it, normalize it, make it fashionable and "cool" and even heroic, and ironically they use their God-given talents to do so.

They sit far above the rest of society with the power to wield and interpret law, pass legislation and peddle falsehoods in books, magazines, music, on the Internet, in television shows and movies. They spread lies on social media and attempt to weaken (if not completely break down) church doctrine. They brainwash little children during their earliest school years and continue the indoctrination right on through the years of higher education.

They can pressure businesses, government agencies and social organizations to standardize their twisted lifestyles into formal policies, edicts and programs. They will use the national news media not only to spread their hatred of God's laws and promote their self-destructive behavior and ideas, but also to crush opponents who disagree and stand in their way.

They will solicit law enforcement, courts and bureaucrats to compel people to conform to their godforsaken social mores, standards and even language. They will pressure family members, friends, relatives and even young children to shame those who are found out of compliance with sin until they finally break down and comply.

These are the cliff dwellers, the beasts who could care less that society is being swallowed up in death and drowning in waves of their toxic filth. They know their lies are killing and harming people, but in their lofty position they count it as part and parcel of being their influential and elevated selves. They see the statistics, but they do not make any connection or simply do not care. They live only to see their own godless behavior validated through the complicity of others, rather than caring one atom about the welfare of victims being lead into shame. The fact that others envy and imitate their lifestyles disguises their own wickedness as something that is admired, normal, respectable, liberating and full of merit.

"While they promise them liberty, they themselves are slaves
of corruption." (2 Pet. 2:19 NASB)

God tells them they are doing wrong. His laws are written onto their hearts:

"That which is known about God is evident within them; for
God made it evident to them." (Rom. 1:19 NASB)

But they ignore God and sin's guilt and find comfort that others have been converted to "their reckless, wild living," and they "heap abuse" on those who disagree. (1 Pet. 4:4) They aspire to be called brave, daring and pioneering. The overwhelming societal acceptance—even celebration—of their sins masks for them any pangs that might arise from God-induced remorse. It obscures any need to wash away their sins, even if they are watching others being washed away by those very sins. It gives rise to the conviction that previous generations have gotten it all wrong:

"They became futile in their speculations, and their foolish
heart was darkened. Professing to be wise, they became
fools." (Rom. 1:21 NASB)

If the followers of these beastly guides are destroyed or killed by having bought into this sin, their lives will not have been sacrificed without good cause, the cliff-dwellers believe. Their deaths and illnesses will give rise to breakthroughs in medical science—an assortment of new pills, shots and treatments—that can save others, much in the way Naloxone was invented (and is now carried by most emergency workers and paramedics) to save people from their own reckless, despair-induced opioid overdoses.

These "leaders" exemplify the scripture: "They are blind guides of the blind. And if a blind man guides a blind man, both will fall into a pit." (Matt. 15:14 NASB)

"Professing to be wise," the Apostle Paul says, "they became fools." (Rom. 1:22 NASB)

It is Left in Our Hands

The big questions with which we are left are, "What can I do? How am I supposed to respond? What is my role in all this?"

It might be difficult for us to understand or comprehend, but God does not intervene in these people's foolishness. He expects Christians, the guardians of Truth, to provide that intervention. He wants those of us who bear the Truth to be the light and salt for their salvation. What God does, the Bible tells us, is nothing. He gives these fools over to their desires.

> "Therefore God gave them over in the lusts of their hearts to impurity, so that their bodies would be dishonored among them." (Rom. 1:24 NASB)

They have exchanged the truth for a lie. (Rom.1:25) They looked at God's creation (rather than the Creator Himself) in their futile attempt to discover moral truth. (Rom. 1:26) They dismiss the written word of God in exchange for what science, nature, raw desire and human intellect can teach them. They have abandoned God—and if the church is not there to provide light to see that truth, as well as salt to preserve that truth—God will give them over to their base desires.

> "And just as they did not see fit to acknowledge God any longer, God gave them over to a depraved mind, to do those things which are **not proper** ..." (Rom. 1:28 NASB, emphasis added)

Those "not proper" things weaken the fabric of society and we see their crippling effects everywhere we look—death, hardship, illness, grief and fear.

> "... *being filled with all unrighteousness, wickedness, greed, evil; full of envy, murder, strife, deceit, malice; they are gossips, slanderers, haters of God, insolent, arrogant, boastful, inventors of evil, disobedient to parents, without understanding, untrustworthy, unloving, unmerciful; and although they know the ordinance of God, that those who practice such things are worthy of death, they not only do the same,* **but also give hearty approval to those who practice them.**" *(Rom. 1:28-32, NASB emphasis added)*

That is quite a list. The Apostle Paul makes special mention at the end to draw attention to those who "give hearty approval to those who practice them." They are the cliff dwellers in my dream. They are the poison in the waters; the vile promoters of unrighteousness; the sleazy defenders of wickedness, the miserable inventors of evil. Their goal is to suppress the truth and exchange it for a lie: *The unborn child is not human, it is a fetus; the biological boy is not necessarily a male, he can be female by choice; man was not created by God but evolved from apes or fish; God does not exist, or if He did He is now dead; man is not born in sin, he is born with a clean heart; plants are not simply vegetation, they have a "right to life."* The list of truths that have been exchanged for lies is endless among the "haters of God."

God has a special fury reserved for those who subvert the truth:

> *"For the wrath of God is revealed from heaven against all ungodliness and unrighteousness of men* **who suppress the truth** *in unrighteousness." (Rom. 1:18, NASB emphasis added)*

Wrath awaits those who "crush the truth." (CEV)

It will be futile for them to try and appease God with conciliatory hand gestures, as I witnessed in my dream. "They are without excuse," the Apostle Paul says. (Rom. 1:20 NASB) "For even though they knew God, they did not honor Him as God or give thanks." (Rom. 1:21 NASB) God's eyes will be focused on these purveyors of evil. He knows who they are and will not be bought off.

As the Prophet Zephaniah warned, "Neither their silver nor their gold shall be able to deliver them in the day of the LORD'S wrath." (Zep. 1:18)

> *"But the eyes of the wicked will fail, and there will be **no escape** for them; And their hope is to breathe their last." (Job 11:20 NASB, emphasis added)*

The doom of these people is foretold, but what about Christians living in this sinful world? Can they avoid this carnage? As much as Christians may like to believe they will be spared from these evil waves—the product of depraved minds—they are wholly mistaken. In fact, many Christians will not even see the destroying waves coming, as was the case in my dream when I questioned a Christian friend who was oblivious to the calamity approaching his doorstep.

Christians in the Path of Destruction

This type of destruction is not for evildoers alone. Christians will be, and have been, caught up in the perilous power of these crashing, indiscriminate waves. This should inspire all Christians never to abandon being the light and salt of the Earth—our true calling.

> *"When the righteous triumph, there is great glory, **but when the wicked rise, men hide themselves**." (Proverbs 28:12 NASB, emphasis added)*

When evil prevails people want to run from its death, illness, harm and misery. Already there are countless ways Christians have been caught up in the tidal wave of evil, mostly through no fault of their own.

Christians have been victims of church shootings. Christian families have been torn apart over the loss of a loved one from an overdose, or a family member getting an abortion, or a predator molesting their son or daughter. You can be a Christian and still get tripped, kicked or punched in the face by a complete stranger "just for fun." Syphilis, gonorrhea and even HIV can be contracted without having illicit sex. Just because you are a Christian does not mean you can't be robbed or murdered for your car, your money, even your shoes. Christians, like anyone else, can be scammed, gunned down by a terrorist or caught in the middle of gang violence.

Christians have been the victims of kidnapping, rape, drive-by shootings and other random violence and malice. Consumer products these days have tamper-proof seals, since evil lunatics have proven they will indiscriminately kill people by poisoning their food or medicines.

When mass murderer Stephen Paddock opened fire on a crowd of concertgoers from a hotel window during the Harvest Music Festival in Las Vegas in 2017, he did not distinguish between Christian and non-Christian. Fifty-nine people died and 363 were wounded.

The same could be said about the evil terror attacks on the World Trade Center and Pentagon in 2001, which targeted Americans, yet killed people of many different nationalities. It is true of many other terrorist attacks before and since (although it must be pointed out that in many cases, Christians have in fact been singled out for attack or death.)

Since 2015, 178 children have been either shot or knifed to death in American schools, with assailants not caring less whether the victims were Christians. And who can forget the millions of innocent unborn babies that have been murdered since 1973? How many of those individuals could have gone on to happy, fulfilling Christian lives?

Virtually everywhere we go we are reminded that evil people have the potential to kill us. We pass through annoying, embarrassing security checks at airports, sporting events, concerts, theaters and amusement parks. We see guards stationed at train stations, stores, businesses, housing developments, schools and parks.

Whether criminal or not, Christian or not, in today's world everyone is now treated as a suspect with possible harmful intentions. You can be invasively frisked, have your belongings searched, be forced to show identification, be electronically scanned, questioned or asked to strip just to gain entry into commonplace public services, events or transportation.

There is so much evil in the world, and precautions are so strict, that authorities felt compelled to arrest a 10-year-old boy for bringing a toy gun into a Northern Virginia school while a 16-year-old was arrested for having a small pocketknife inside a Harrison County, Miss. school.

So the tidal wave of evil does not distinguish between Christians and evildoers. Though it is crashing all around us—we see it, feel it, live in it—many Christians willfully turn a blind eye and refuse to confront it with the only solution that can redeem society: being the salt and the light to the world.

The "world" recognizes the consequences of evil, but is not willing to change. It relies on a host of Band-Aid treatments to stem, slow down and temporarily dam the flood—the potential carnage arising from these frightful waves of destruction.

Which Band-Aid treatments? They are all around us: Security and surveillance are being amped up throughout the world. Medical research is being increased. More rehab centers are being funded and psychiatric treatment centers are becoming more ubiquitous and affordable. Firearms availability and free speech, both such important parts of a free and law-abiding existence, are being curtailed. Clean, free needles are being offered to make illegal drug use "safer." Condoms are being handed out to schoolchildren at no cost to make indiscriminate, illicit sex "safer." Why? Because the consequences of full-blown sin bring unavoidable illness and death and crime, and billions of dollars must be spent—as well as freedoms taken away—to mitigate these effects.

Yet as every Christian should know, if sin is not honestly confronted at its root level—that is, the human denial of God—these finger-in-the-dam solutions are doomed to failure. The dam will soften, crack, and break. As described above, Christians will be caught up along with everyone else in the waves of destruction and death.

Is Being Deemed 'Worthy' Enough to Escape?

So again … what do we do and where do we go? How do we find safety? Where do we hide? *Should* we hide?

The Psalmist David wanted to hide when the "pressure of the wicked" surrounded him. (Ps. 55:3) He spoke of the "terrors of death" and its "horror" when "iniquity and mischief" cause "destruction in the land." Not unlike today, he was surrounded by "oppression and deceit" and "bloodshed" in the streets.

His only desire was to "wander off" and hasten his "escape from the windy storm and tempest." (Ps. 55:8) He pleaded with God to "cause me to escape."

> *"Deliver me, O my God, out of the hand of the wicked, out of the hand of the unrighteous and cruel man." (Ps. 71:4)*

Escaping the torrential flood of sin that will grant no mercy to the lives in its path may seem impossible, with each route of escape wrapped in smoke so thick it is impossible to see, let alone know what is on the other side. When Noah was told to escape the "widespread wickedness of the earth," he had but one option: Build an ark. That is hardly an option for us today, though some people still try.

Yet we have no choice but to escape if we do not want to be swallowed up by these deadly waves of sin. But will God consider us "worthy" of escaping?

> *"Watch ye therefore, and pray always, that ye may be **accounted worthy to escape all these things** that shall come to pass, and to stand before the Son of man." (Luke 21:36, emphasis added)*

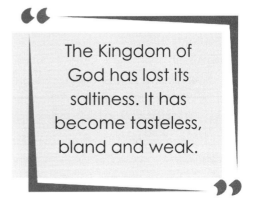

> The Kingdom of God has lost its saltiness. It has become tasteless, bland and weak.

There is that word again: *worthy*. In this case it means to be "judged worthy." That is, to possess worth and value. The way to have "worth," as we have discussed, is to take up the cross. The words of Christ bear repeating here: "And he who does not take his cross and follow after Me **is not worthy of Me**." (Matt. 10:38, emphasis added)

Remember it. Write it down. Repeat it to yourself.

The team of police officers I saw in the dream, just after emerging from that dense cloud of smoke, should be considered a checkpoint of *worthiness* in our lives.

Are we "accounted worthy to escape?" It means more than calling on the name of the Lord, or doing good works, or forsaking sin, or being a prayer warrior, or even performing miracles.

To be worthy means to "take up the cross" *while doing these things.* It means the willingness to forsake everything—including mother, father, sons and daughters—for Jesus Christ.

> *"He that loveth father or mother more than me **is not worthy of me**: and he that loveth son or daughter more than me is **not worthy of me**." (Matt. 10:37, emphasis added)*

Being counted worthy is not complicated, except to those who would rather hold onto their riches and worldly connections than take up the cross and defend the Word of God.

> *"So that we ourselves glory in you in the churches of God for your patience and faith in **all your persecutions and tribulations that ye endure**: Which is a manifest token of the righteous judgment of God, that **ye may be counted worthy** of the kingdom of God, for which ye also suffer." (2 Thes. 1:4-5, emphasis added)*

No one should think that "suffering," "persecution," or "tribulation" come only at the point of a gun, in chains or while facing cumbersome lawsuits. Taking up the cross rarely results in death, jail or court—at least in the United States. It does mean having the willingness to lose what you have (whether precious or small) to stand for Christ. Many former Muslims have lost fathers, mothers, sons and daughters after converting to Christianity. Some Christians have lost jobs, such as actors in Hollywood who refused certain roles or shooting certain scenes on moral grounds. Others have lost businesses, such as the owners of a bridal shop in Bloomsburg, Pa., that was forced to shut its doors after refusing to provide services for same-sex weddings.

Sometimes taking up the cross is no more than standing firm when being shunned by peers or co-workers, or being made the butt of jokes, or being attacked in the media.

One thing is certain, however. No one will ever have to take up the cross if he cannot handle being the salt and the light to the world. If people are not willing to be a light to the world so others can find their way to the Truth, if they are not willing to be the salt in the world to preserve that truth, then there could hardly be any occasion to "take up the cross," could there?

In 2019, the Public Religion Research Institute published the results of a shocking survey that found 57 percent of Christians *agreeing* that it should be illegal for other Christians to deny services to homosexual weddings. It is doubtful these squishy and "lukewarm" Christians will ever face the opportunity to take up the cross. But they are worthy of Christ spitting them out of His mouth. (Rev. 3:16)

The Salt and the Light

This combination of *salt* and *light* is what constitutes our refuge and safety. It is where Christ lives. We will never know how to escape to it without taking up the cross in our Christian journey. It encompasses the Kingdom of God. We are its defenders, its protectors. There are those who want to destroy it, with violence and force if necessary, which they have been doing since the time of John the Baptist.

> *"From the days of John the Baptist until now the kingdom of heaven suffers violence, and violent men take it by force." (Matt. 11:12 NASB)*

A tidal wave of evil threatens all of us. Christians are in its path just like everyone else. It can't be escaped via medicine, science, psychiatrists, humanist philosophy, drugs or concocted religions.

And it certainly cannot be prevented through Christian passivity, fatalism, seclusion or silence.

"The Lord is a warrior," Moses and Miriam wrote in a song. (Ex. 15:3 NASB) And He "will go forth like a warrior," Isaiah tells us. "He will arouse His zeal like a man of war. He will utter a shout, yes, He will raise a war cry. (Is. 42:13 NASB) In the end, He will be a "victorious warrior," says Zephaniah. (Zep. 3:17 NASB)

Christ has chosen you and me to be soldiers in His army, led by the ultimate warrior, Christ Himself. It will involve hardship, which we must endure patiently as we carry that cross of passion. Our ultimate goal in being soldiers—being a light, being the salt, being a Christian on Earth—is for Christ's kingdom, which is in our midst.

> *"But if I cast out devils by the Spirit of God, then **the kingdom of God is come unto you.**" (Matt. 12:28, emphasis added)*

The kingdom is here. It is upon us. Christ gave the keys to that kingdom to Peter. (Matt. 16:19) It is the Rock of Christ. But Christ also cautioned Peter:

> *"Whatsoever thou shalt bind on earth shall be bound in heaven: and whatsoever thou shalt loose on earth shall be loosed in heaven." (Matt. 16:19)*

Are we binding sin on Earth? Or are we allowing sin to run rampant on Earth? If we refuse to be the light and salt, we are not binding anything. The cataclysm of sin, lawlessness, corruption and violence will be without boundaries—and Christians will be in its path.

This is why Christ also warned:

> *"Therefore, salt is good; but if even salt has become tasteless, with what will it be seasoned? It is useless either for the soil or for the manure pile; it is thrown out. He who has ears to hear, let him hear." (Luke 14: 34-35 NASB)*

And elsewhere:

> *"You are the salt of the earth; but if the salt has become tasteless, how can it be made salty again? It is no longer good for anything, except to be thrown out and trampled under foot by men." (Matt: 5:13 NASB)*

Everywhere we look we see God's Word being "thrown out and trampled under foot by men." We know why, because the Bible tells us why. The Kingdom of God has lost its saltiness. It has become tasteless, bland and weak. When that happens, it is good neither for the "soil" (meaning Christian believers) nor for the "manure pile" (non-believers).

In his book *Walk On,* Ben Malcolmson relates a personal story. Malcolmson, director of external relations for the Seattle Seahawks, tells of an incident when he decided to hand out Bibles to his football teammates while at the University of Southern California.

"I got an idea after reading Isaiah 55. It says in there that 'If His word goes out, it does not return empty,' " Malcolmson told the *Christian Post.* "It hit me that we need to put His word out there."

He placed Bibles on the locker room seats of each teammate. He did it on Christmas Eve. When he returned, however, every Bible lay torn apart on the floor.

"Everywhere I looked, shredded tissue-thin pages of the Bibles were strewn upon the floor, so much that I could hardly see even a sliver of the cardinal carpet," he wrote. "I stood frozen in place as my heart sank and I felt the blood drain from my face. Never in any of my daydreams had I envisioned a scene like this," Malcolmson said.

There was God's word: Discarded, torn apart, thrown on the floor. Literally trampled underfoot by men—men with cleats on.

We know the "gates of hell shall not prevail against" the Kingdom of Heaven, God's church. (Matt. 16:18) Jesus has promised us that. That does not mean men will not trample His Word under foot, however.

Not Broken, Only Brought Low

As an example, for decades the United States modeled American exceptionalism to the rest of the world. We proudly displayed our freedom, constitution, liberties, generosity, non-expansionist power, egalitarianism and individualism. We encouraged others to accept our ways of government, economics, morality, citizenry and liberty.

But during the 1970s, in the dark shadow of the Vietnam War, American exceptionalism came under attack from within and without. Whereas America was once touted as a "City on a Hill" for other nations to admire and imitate, it began to be painted as evil and Satanic by a growing number of countries … and influential Americans. American exceptionalism began to be trampled underfoot.

Chelsea Clinton, daughter of Bill and Hillary, has said, "Every day at some point I encounter some sort of anti-America feeling."

We continue to see that anti-American sentiment promoted at sporting events, in the streets, in movies, in the news and in song.

It will take more than trying to trample American exceptionalism to bring down the United States of America, however. America's bones remain strong.

Nor will Satan not prevail against the Kingdom of God. That does not mean the Lord's truths won't be trampled upon—muting our message, impugning our beliefs, damaging our credibility, frustrating our mission and miring the glory of Christ's resurrection and salvation in falsehoods and noise.

Christ has chosen us. As soldiers of Christ, who bear the cross daily, we must be prepared to engage. Rather than letting our message be trampled on and thrown aside, we need to be trampling the ideas of the wicked and reducing them to ashes. Our goal is to crush Satan under OUR feet.

> "You will tread down the wicked, for they will be ashes under the soles of your feet on the day which I am preparing,' says the LORD of hosts." (Mal. 4:3 NASB)

> "The God of peace will soon crush Satan under your feet. The grace of our Lord Jesus be with you." (Rom. 16:20 NASB)

Not an Ending, but a Beginning

The title of the next book in this series contains two words that should ring very familiar by now. It is called: *Salt and Light*. It will go far in answering those looming questions of *What should I do?* and *Where should I go?* Learn more about the responsibility of Christians to bind evil, subdue and rule the Earth without apology or reservation, preserve and proclaim the truth. Learn more about who the Enemy is and all its different forms, from secularism to feminism to militant Islam. Learn how to confront and conquer that enemy—sometimes using his own strategies— without becoming like him or becoming something otherwise displeasing to God.

Look at your own country, for as an American you are an already part of the Earth's first and greatest Christian nation.

Most importantly, learn to look at your own self, your own talents and strengths and gifts, and see the ways you can play a meaningful role in the struggle to come.

You have your helmet, shield, belt, sword and shoes. Let the training continue.